Sons of My Skin

By Peter Redgrove

The Collector and Other Poems
Routledge & Kegan Paul

The Nature of Cold Weather and Other Poems
Routledge & Kegan Paul

At the White Monument and Other Poems
Routledge & Kegan Paul

The Force and Other Poems
Routledge & Kegan Paul

Work in Progress
(Poems 1969)

The Hermaphrodite Album
(with Penelope Shuttle)

Dr Faust's Sea-Spiral Spirit and Other Poems
Routledge & Kegan Paul

In the Country of the Skin
Routledge & Kegan Paul

The Terrors of Dr Treviles
(with Penelope Shuttle)
Routledge & Kegan Paul

Sons of My Skin

Redgrove's Selected Poems 1954—1974

CHOSEN AND INTRODUCED BY
Marie Peel

Routledge & Kegan Paul
London and Boston

First published in 1975
by Routledge & Kegan Paul Ltd
Broadway House, 68–74 Carter Lane,
London EC4V 5EL and
9 Park Street,
Boston, Mass. 02108, USA
Set in Bembo
and printed in Great Britain by the Alden Press, Oxford
The poems © Peter Redgrove
1959 The Collector and Other Poems
1961 The Nature of Cold Weather and Other Poems
1963 At the White Monument and Other Poems
1966 The Force and Other Poems
1968 "The Agnostic Visitor"
1969 "Hush! The Sun"
1972 Dr Faust's Sea-Spiral Spirit and Other Poems,
"Nine Sorceries", "The Son of My Skin", "Beyond the
Eyelids" and "The Jesus Apparition"
1973 In the Country of the Skin, The Hermaphrodite
Album and "A Philosophy in Welshese"
This collection © Peter Redgrove 1975
Introduction © Marie Peel 1975

ISBN 0 7100 8073 5 (C)
0 7100 8074 3 (P)

Contents

The Force and Other Poems (1966)

Introduction

by Marie Peel

Most writers of strong originality see and feel ahead of their time. They usually dig deep also in ways that show our constant loss in wholeness and energy through conforming compromise. Most readers shrink from the glare and heat of such vision. They shut their ears to its whispering undermining explosiveness. They prefer interpretations that confirm and protect their own view of things, often seeking to impose this on the writer. But important writers are uncompromising and cannot be manipulated in this way.

I think Peter Redgrove is a writer of this stature and that the time has come for this to be more fully recognized. Still in his early forties, he has already published six volumes of poetry as well as a number of dramatic pieces and two unusual compelling novels. He is strongly prolific. But while he has achieved considerable recognition, I do not think this is primarily, as yet for the vision that is there. Reading one or two poems, one is almost certainly struck by his strange memorable quality. Reading further within one volume, one may feel some resistance to the restless fantasy, the constant changes of identity, the startling difficulties or seeming incoherence that shoots out and swirls around one.

This is why I think it adds immensely to his impact to read him more consecutively in a chronological selection such as is offered here. Then one finds a growing understanding in response, with each poem important in and for itself, but also connecting within and across the books as part of a developing whole. A dialectical whole that is nowhere near completion yet. One's own vision sharpens, grows more adventurous and elastic and then, suddenly, the poet's powerful startling coherence breaks through. Leaps up, thrusts into and empowers one's own imagination. For here is a writer deeply engaged with life and poetry in an interlocking, many-layered way. At times this takes him deep into the physical universe and man's collective unconscious. At others he flares forth, touching with probing power the infinite surface of life, the stretched skin, as it were, of the natural world or of himself as an individual human being.

Poetry of this order needs recognition to match its own inner and outer penetration and it needs this as the poet writes, not in his old age or, as with Blake, a century and a half after his death. For recognition and response contribute to the poet's power, they help him make his own truest future poetry. Also I would say that our society needs the myth-making power of such poetry as a source of energy and vision with which to make its future.

I mention Blake deliberately for he and Peter Redgrove share a knowledge of poetry as articulate energy, and of energy as the source of all creative power. "Eternal delight", Blake called it. He also said that all man's ideas of God or gods "reside in the human breast". Peter Redgrove would agree with this, as he would I think with another of Blake's central convictions: "Everything that lives is holy". But he goes behind Blake with an animistic vision of science that precedes Newton and flares ahead of Darwin. Materialism does not have to be single-visioned and dead. Only those with a strong vested interest in propping up the Christian God call it this. For Peter Redgrove the power and pattern of existence are essentially inherent in the natural world, they are embedded and flowing there. In this sense he is a materialist, but one for whom—to use his own phrase and emphasis—"matter sings".

There are other unusual combinations in his vision. For at present he is both evolutionary and individualist; not revolutionary and for the generality of men, as Blake was and as I think Keats would have become, the Keats who knew the greatest poets to be those for whom, as he put it in "The Fall of Hyperion": "the miseries of the world/Are misery and will not let them rest."

Peter Redgrove is appalled by these miseries—they were an instinctive part of his rejection of his own privilege—but he did not know them instinctively and for their own sake, as part of the pattern of most people's lives over generations. Everything in his English middle-class background, his education at a minor public school and major ancient university, his education, moreover, as a scientist, prevented his knowing this. It also prevented his knowing that most people need some fuller consciousness of an outward social kind, before they can begin to become fully themselves. His rebellion was essentially *against* consciousness, against what it had done to him through its confident supposed control by his own class. The move for him was irresistibly out, down, away from this form of consciousness towards the unconscious.

Not that he made a conscious choice. It happened. His mind, his whole psyche, the country of his skin, knew with appalling intensity the effects of this divide-and-rule philosophy with its opposition of body and mind, its denial of Eros, its emphasis on thrusting masculine drive at the expense of nurturing female creativeness. He recoiled also from the castration of knowledge with every sliver labelled for analysis rather than the living continuum he knew, with no distinction in kind between chemistry and geology and psychology and music and poetry or any other study. Every part of him rejected this dividedness and recorded its effects with extraordinary energy. This produced strong disruptions in his mental and emotional life. It also produced his poetry.

The evolutionary drive of his rejection seems to have been compulsion—perhaps one could better say *impulsion*—towards non-human nature, the life of the earth and stars and flowing spirit of water. It was essentially away from houses and mansions, symbols of man's need to domesticate himself within the universe. Also (if one has been brought up to believe Christ's teaching: "In my Father's house are many mansions") of his attempt to domesticate himself in an after-life as well. It was essentially away also from the particular house, the home, its shut-in quality for him, the brittle toast-thin living, the woman:

fluffed on the man's arm
Like a floss of him, and he an elbow of her,

while all the time within the hooded pearly whelk of the pram lurked the third pair of staring eyes.

Getting out from all this involved unknowing, a *de*creation, a toppling down the storeys of the traditional hierarchy of creation, so that the poet sees and feels with small ground creatures, inhabits trees and woods and stones as well as knowing power in the strata deep below. Once gone there is no holding him, though they drag the lake of the house for evidence of a corpse. He has a sense of glee and freedom in his power to elude his searchers. He delights in coming back, "the colour of ghosts", but with new substantiality, to lick "every corner where I was/To know as I was known." One has no sense of his being pursued or possessed in this process, but rather of swirling manifold being moving out from fixed positions to those of "no conclusions". But the gleeful freedom is often crossed by pain and sense of loss and above all by bewilderment that the nature of his experience should be so utterly not understood by those closest to him.

An essential element of this experience was the descent deep beneath domesticated surface morality to the heat and power at the core of existence. Here the poet knows an *Ur*-morality where conventional distinctions between good and evil disappear in the fusion of creation, burning up traditional moral and emotional layers accumulated over centuries of Christianity. In the magma at the centre, where power puts its finger, "the lines show thick roots of hot blood" that force new creation. Though infinitely minor compared with the actuality of geology, in his own workings, when there is this hot thick-rooted pressure, the poet knows access of power directly corresponding to it.

The quotations I have given come from poems central to this central experience: from the title poem to the volume, "The Nature of Cold Weather", and from "Power", "Decreator", and "The Absolute Ghost", all in the important fourth book, *The Force and Other Poems*. I could have chosen other poems, especially "Lazarus and the Sea" from the poet's first book, *The Collector*. But in a sense it does not matter which one chooses for all are aspects of the process at the heart of Peter Redgrove's poetry, that also forms its living skin. Once this is known, one can freely inhabit the varied strata of his poems, stretched deep or lying close beneath the surface like layers of the same skin.

One enters autobiographical strata at different levels, knowing the poet as a boy, relationships within his family, the death of a brother, experience in advertising, a visit to Spain. Most deeply embedded and also most intensively recurrent on the surface is a marriage and all that that then meant. Other allegorical figures join the Decreator and the Absolute Ghost to bear witness from different angles to the poet's drowning-into-life. For instance Mr Waterman (in "The Nature of Cold Weather"), who tells a psychiatrist about it; and the Minister in "The Sermon" (in *The Force and Other Poems*), who is tempted by his congregation to reveal the secret of godhead and when he preaches immanence, a shard of power in each of us, is assaulted for his truthfulness.

Significant symbols emerge from the allegory. More than once a white-haired old man appears, a blind gardening God the Father, endlessly tending a tamed Mother Earth. He is for ever hedging and clipping and hypothesizing, dividing body and mind, black earth of matter and white light of spirit, and so is drained of living power, which springs only from some fusion of the two. Black and white often recur symbolically as night and day or as symbolic colours in a sexual context, while there is often a similar rich interconnection between sun and moon.

As I have suggested, there are deep geological strata, particularly in the poem, "The Nature of Cold Weather", with its manifestation of heat shut up and pressed down within the frozen universe. We see the beauty of the surface under ice moved back to an extinct ice age. Then there is fresh snow, the swirling movement of it, followed by intense painful pricking of the thaw felt across the poet's whole being as he inhabits the landscape. In "Minerals of Cornwall, Stones of Cornwall", in the poet's most recent volume, *Dr Faust's Sea-Spiral Spirit*, the image of a white kaolin-station steams deep within the moor, empowering future ages in the gleaming fixed "inclusions" of the rocks; moving also with infinite slowness towards "good conclusions" up above, in the free seeding of the millennia. Other poems are alight with the chemistry and physics of the universe, the beaming power of the sun, the power in water and electricity and in man's human beam, the life-force of his sexual energy.

All these poems spring from the self of the poet, who has utterly lived his own remark "he is dead who cannot change utterly". Before, he was the interested naturalist of "The Collector", with his "reasonable curiosity", and "observations in default of love". Now he becomes the man in "I See" (in the *Force* volume), loving the natural world in a new way that knows it utterly for itself and for his own relatedness to its processes. He sees the bug embracing a grass-bole, its "mouth-awls working with excitement for the plunge,/And he sees it fuss back again stout with its eggs". He also sees himself, the boy he was, the man he is, spitting a cherrystone into a weedclump, "believing it will spring/Of his mouth, having warmed it and started the small germ moving".

But no one can live wholly and powerfully through the non-human natural world alone. One must have natural human living as well and in this sphere the reborn poet is driven by less fruitful contraries. The Widower, for instance, in the poem of that name, knows what he has done to his wife, a woman who was "daytime to the mind", to whom he brought: "Twelve-hour lyings down for fear of this world". The poem is full of the contraries of day and night, the night full of self-induced, self-justifying fears. Its vision of life grows morbid, "the too-great majority" walking like "a shivering laundry of shifted humanity/And who stink. . . ." The poet quickly repudiates this false emphasis, spawned by the inbreeding of night thoughts, and turns towards the evolutionary truth of day. Here the vision is no longer the Christian humanist one of the great chain of being leading up to God the Father, which could make a man like Hamlet cry in pain: "What should such fellows as I do crawling between heaven and earth?" Rather, on a shorn bristly lawn, "full of mentality", the poet honours the creature for itself:

The spires and sinews of the worm, how excellent!
Dragging the long cold chain of life for itself,
And the cold speed of its terror,
And the drops of itself massaging into the corridor.

But evolutionary vision must be aware of change and of progression through change. All life needs night as well as day for growth. They are true contraries in Blake's sense when he wrote: "Without Contraries is no Progression". But if the psyche is severely disturbed some contraries easily become fixed opposites that entrap and shut one in instead of resolving and setting free. By the end of the poem one may feel the Widower is entrapped in his new freedom. He himself was dead, is now alive, which by too tight a logic turns an unchanged wife into a dead one, himself into a kind of murderer. Looked at more dialectically, the wife must have changed also because of him, as he has done in part because of her.

The poet's rebirth expresses itself in a new range of poetic *personae*, going beneath and beyond Christianity: Taliessin, the Welsh poet, disciple of Merlin, who sought different voices and congenial forms to express the manifold knowing of his imagination; Frankenstein, the modern Prometheus, who created not static perfection, but the suffering complexity of human life; above all Faust, whose Sea-Spiral in the title poem of the last book, *Dr Faust's Sea-Spiral Spirit*, comes sweeping in from the sea, drawing up power and releasing it in everything it touches. The driving force of Goethe is very strong here, a great poet and original scientist for whom our culture has no equivalent because of its static division between arts and sciences, though I think Peter Redgrove will help to change this.

In Goethean science imagination is essential, the scientist must enter the trees and rocks and plants he studies, must know deeply in himself something of the forces working in the universe. For Goethe colours were not made by refraction of white light solely, but by interpenetration of darkness with light, they are equal though different forces. Newton's interpretation, which our culture chose, stresses what the poet calls "exclusive masculinity", the thrust of abstract intellect divorced from deeper knowing. The powerful Earth-Spirit of Part I of Goethe's *Faust* goes far towards accepting the contrary energies of life in all its forms. In Part II there is no one all-powerful Sea-Spirit to equal this, but two elusive spirits both of whom, one senses, would make a strong appeal to Peter Redgrove: Thales, the earliest known Greek philosopher, who taught that the world was made of water; and Proteus, "the Carpathian wizard", as Milton called him, capable of infinite transformation.

Peter Redgrove's Sea-Spiral Spirit infuses and is infused through all the elements. Spiralling across the world, it lifts up and is lifted up by a fifth, the whirling doughnut of energy the physicists call plasma, that creates force at the core of everything:

It hums like a top and its voice smashes volcanoes,
Yet it will burrow and from the riflings of Etna
Speed skyward, hurtling pillar of red rock.

In Cornwall, where the poet lives, it "electrifies Perranporth sand-dunes" so that every grain "crackles and hums" beneath his slippered feet. As they embrace, men and women impersonate it, they are "a cone of power/An unbuilt beehive". This spiralling spirit does not find the Earth-Spirit too ugly, it knows the spellbound containment of its power within the earth and Faust's own power of spells to call it up.

A parallel poem, "The Haunted Armchair", finally lays the spirit of the jobbing gardener who was God the Father. A voice comes from the chair, itself evocative of gentlemen's libraries, leather-bound volumes, abstract power of mind. Still dividing body and mind, it wants to go on doing so until the end of time.

Until, suddenly, a strong new sense of time comes in, which is also immeasurably old, and undermines the man-made separation. He hears time flowing, "time eroding, the cinder withering in the grate". "How much time," he asks, "have I seen withering?" Then suddenly there is release, not into death but into ever-evolving life, as he proclaims: "Suddenly everything *grants* me withering" (my italics).

The personal allegory completing this extraordinary trinity comes through "The Idea of Entropy at Maenporth Beach", which though not specifically written as such is a direct answer to Wallace Stevens's fine romantic poem, "The Idea of Order at Key West". In this sea and sky are given order and meaning for the poet by the beauty of the girl's song. Peter Redgrove endorses the creative power of the artist acknowledged here, but he knows that waves and sky have meaning in themselves, have energy and evolutionary power, however random and boring their incredibly slow process is to restless trapped romantics. His white singer enters the disorderly mud, "From this collision were new colours born" and new power for the poet.

Since his *Faust* book, Peter Redgrove's directions have been many and full of developing contraries, with the prose poems of his novels becoming increasingly important to him. His power has always been a strongly dramatizing one, in the tradition of medieval morality, dramatizing warring elements in the self rather than springing from dramatic absorption in the lives of others. His "Three Pieces for Voices" seems to form a dramatic trinity matching the three poems in the *Faust* book, with the first, "The Son of My Skin", recasting God the Father as the Emperor who gives his only begotten self to be flayed alive for humanity's sake and then is radiantly set apart in men's eyes as the Emperor's son. "The Jesus Apparition" re-enacts the Ascension as a Descension or Extension of total being, while "Beyond the Eyelids", with its epigraph from E. T. A. Hoffmann's tale, *Rath Krespel*, dramatizes personal experience of the poet knowing himself a protective skin-of-the-eyeball short in intensity of seeing. His novel, *In the Country of the Skin*, extends this hyper-awareness to the skin of the whole body which, when one lives with any conflicting intensity, always records this in its own strange way. The book presents the central experiences of the poet's life I have been referring to, as they happen, in a startlingly direct way and deserves to be read entire for itself. The excerpt in this volume is from the more consciously constructed radio version.

In Peter Redgrove's more recent poetry there is no longer a sense of marking time in shut-in domesticity, as in a poem like "Sweat", for instance, in *The Force and Other Poems*. Nor of further discoveries of the liberating evolutionary power of time. Instead there is often a joyous offering of the present time, a celebration of unique personal living, an absorption in poetry as spell and ritual. The experience behind this clearly releases powers in the poet, but this does not always make the poetry powerful for others. People need powerful art to energize them for their own living, they don't need that living done for them and in a sense that is what any ritualizing of experience is. The prose poem, "Really Gone" (in *The Force and Other Poems*), suggests that Peter Redgrove intuitively knows this and that no art can be a substitute for full and satisfying living. The contraries of his own experience up till that time leap out at one from every page in the *Faust* book, with a poem like "Tell Me, Doctor", for instance, revealing the continuing life of a relationship supposed dead; "Half-Scissors", the flashing cutting dependence of one very much alive. Some of his poetry since then ignores this contrary, producing its own shut-in ritualistic quality even when enacted out of doors. One misses the cool clear note of the outside world for its own sake, which the poet himself sounds in "Directive", written earlier in answer to "Sweat". Indoors it is at times as if Mr Looking-Glass has succeeded Mr Waterman, with flashing mirrors to look sideways at, rather than doors opening to pass through.

Recent uncollected poems already begin to refute this, showing a new power to enter other people as distinct from divers aspects of himself, or others seen only in relation to himself; and "From the Questions to Mary" is a new bringing together of Greek and Christian traditions. The last poem selected for this volume, "From the Reflections of Mr Glass", has a renewal of his original fresh flowing quality, a pursuit of light rather than darkness and so perhaps a movement towards release from any jig-saw puzzle of correspondences for their own sake. In this short excerpt one senses new hope of bringing back to life what has seemed dead. "However dark it is," the poet writes, "there is enough light/To gather within your darkness like a seed of light."

As I said earlier, Peter Redgrove has spoken of himself as one for whom "matter *sings*". This is so with the poetry also, the song is very much in the matter, not the manner of it. There is no particular magic in the artistry, no particular outward spell of rhyme or stanza pattern to enact meaning. But there is tremendous store of inner energy, both in rhythm and imagery. Rhythmically one feels this working in a strongly inner, tidal way, with variations in length of lines, speed of movement, degree of poetic pressure. There is also strong entropic power in the compression of what he images, giving back the germ of life, the particle of force, to have its own effect. The tree, for instance, "preening herself with a soft bough-purr"; "the living lips of the worm nibbling air"; "gulls like airships whose furnace draught is screams". These are only a very few grains from the stuffed granary that is there, to say nothing of the radiant outward-flashing power of many other images.

I have made this selection and write this introduction to express my own vision of the shapes and directions and particular quality of the poet's work so far. He has wanted me to do this. But the free seeding of my choice is in the minds and imaginations of readers, it is what they see and hear and know within, in response to the power of what they read, which I think one finds grows with re-reading. As with the truly poetic in all its forms, there is magic in this process, a fusion of inner and outer power one cannot analyse.

Marie Peel

Acknowledgments

"The Sermon" first appeared on the BBC television programme, *Monitor*, for which it was specially commissioned. "The Son of My Skin" and "Beyond the Eyelids" originally appeared in *Three Pieces for Voices*, published by Poet & Printer, 1972. "The Jesus Apparition", an excerpt from each act of which is given in this volume, was also published in *Three Pieces for Voices* after its original commissioning by the Orchard Players at the Beaford Centre in Devon. The excerpt from *In the Country of the Skin* is from the radio play first broadcast on Radio Three in June 1973. This was a free adaptation by Peter Redgrove from his novel of the same name, which won the 1973 *Guardian* fiction prize. *The Hermaphrodite Album* (published by Fuller D'Arch Smith, 1973) is the fruit of very close poetic conjunction between Peter Redgrove and the poet and novelist, Penelope Shuttle. The poems and prose-poem included in this volume are by Peter Redgrove. "The Agnostic Visitor" appeared in *Penguin Modern Poets 11* (1968). "Hush! The Sun" was in the interim volume, *Work in Progress* (Poet & Printer, 1969). The remaining poems in the "Uncollected Poems" section have all been written since the publication of *Dr Faust's Sea-Spiral Spirit* and have not yet appeared in book form. "A Philosophy in Welshese" was in *Meridian* (4 November 1973); "Nine Sorceries" appeared in the *Scotsman* (30 December 1972); and "From the Reflections of Mr Glass" was circulated during March and April 1974, in *Words: Broadsheet Eight* (© Words Press 1974).

The Collector and
Other Poems

Anniversaire Triste

A piano plays my aunt in a lacquered room;
The wood and ivory lend a dead man sound;
Grinning with grilles, Samurai armour stands
Booming a little with the afterlife.

Her elbows stick out and her face goes down:
This is the climax, the triumphant foe
Death; I remember one tear really flew
And hit a vased rose, and hung there like a dew.

Indeed we all cried: herself, myself, the maid
Called in to listen to it once a year;
Her face came up, her fingers down! she was
    finished now
Labouring to communicate her pain.

She succeeded when she beat me stealing jam.
I found her piano-plaining pleasant, I'm afraid—
My boy's heart was carving with a penknife
A name, a heart, while sap oozed round the blade.

Against Death

We are glad to have birds in our roof
Sealed off from rooms by white ceiling,
And glad to glimpse them homing straight
Blinking across the upstairs windows,
And to listen to them scratching on the laths
As we bed and whisper staring at the ceiling.
We're glad to be hospitable to birds.
In our rooms, in general only humans come,
We keep no cats and dislike wet-mouthed dogs,
And wind comes up the floorboards in a gale,
So then we keep to bed: no more productive place
To spend a blustery winter evening and keep warm.
Occasionally a spider capsizes in the bath,
Blot streaming with legs among the soap,
Cool and scab-bodied, soot-and-suet,
So we have to suffocate it down the pipe
For none of us'd have dealings with it,
Like kissing a corpse's lips, even
Through the fingers, so I flood it out.
In our high-headed rooms we're going to breed
Many human beings for their home
To fill the house with children and with life,
Running in service of the shrill white bodies,
With human life but for sparrows in the roof,
Wiping noses and cleaning up behind,
Slapping and sympathising, and catching glimpses
Of each other and ourselves as we were then,
And let out in the world a homing of adults.

And if there ever should be a corpse in the house
Hard on its bedsprings in a room upstairs,
Smelling of brass-polish, with sucked-in cheeks,

Staring through eyelids at a scratching ceiling,
Some firm'd hurry it outdoors and burn it quick—
We'd expect no more to happen to ourselves
Our children gradually foregoing grief of us
As the hot bodies of the sparrows increase each summer.

Old House

I lay in an agony of imagination as the wind
Limped up the stairs and puffed on the landings,
Snuffled through floorboards from the foundations,
Tottered, withdrew into flaws, and shook the house.
Peppery dust swarmed through all cracks,
The boiling air blew a dry spume from other mouths,
From other hides and function:
Scale of dead people fountained to the ceiling—
What sort of a house is this to bring children to,

Burn it down, build with new-fired brick;
How many times has this place been wound up
Around the offensive memories of a dead person,
Or a palette of sick colours dry on the body,
Or bare arms through a dank trapdoor to shut off water,
Or windows filmed over the white faces of children:
"This is no place to bring children to"

I cried in a nightmare of more
Creatures shelled in bone-white,
Or dead eyes fronting soft ermine faces,
Or mantled in carnation, dying kings of creation,
Or crimson mouth-skirts flashing as they pass:
What a world to bring new lives into,

3

Flat on my back in a warm bed as the house around me
Lived in the wind more than the people that built it;
It was bought with all our earned money,
With all the dust I was nearly flying from my body
That whipped in the wind in this normal November,
And outstretched beside her in my silly agony
She turned in her sleep and called for me,
Then taught me what children were to make a home for.

Aid

I almost popped underfoot
A shiny beetle like a boot
Its laces waving in the air
Not knowing how it was or where;
Being drunk, I had the knack
To know its feelings on its back;
I'd get my foot under its carapace
And shove it safely back to grass:
It might want to get there quick
To the damp grass to be sick
Or, plates creaking, unload its eggs.
I stood unsteady on my bottled legs
And raised one foot, as I have said:
But, to keep my balance, squashed its head.

Looking down, I held my breath
At this accidental death;
Scanning up and down the path,
I waited for descending wrath;

Then, keeping the ground beneath my feet,
I strolled off home to eat,
Along the stony paths, leaf-strewn,
Whistling a sober little tune.

A Leaf from my Bestiary

Swallowing earth through his nose,
The worm inches his miles;
The fine grain at the grassroots stirs
And his limy lips nibble in day—
Then, snap! like a gun, from the high air
The bird's tapping beak is in through the stalks
And worm hurried through height that smarts his
    moist hide,
Rushes into his wounds: to the horrible children
That crash in the twisted nest. These birds
Hoist up the whorled Cellini snail,
Crazing him hak-hak on rocks.

Now why faze the innocent slowcoach worm,
The mother-o'pearl-boned, lip-skirted snail?
Worm's not lazy carrion! he skeins his toil-holes
Lined with worm-sweat. He eats what he finds:
Slides like a train through abominable patches
Or tugs in with all muscles the toothsome leaf.
Snail shaves his salads from stem and leaf.

It is lechery, lechery: fits and starts,
Grabbing and gluttony, while the sightless worm

Like soft successive links of a spring
Wants to pile out and slubber for hours
In the moist slow shade among the twigs
And damn the birds! in this slithing-time.

But if the air is clear, the trees are full;
Birds tread their birds with a hop-snap-tup
Bloody amid a mist of loose feathers—and, safe,
Snail pulls his skull over his ears, to a shriek.

Fiesta

I

Their streets are dry as long bones.
Where they are moist, the vermin meet.
O, won't you give a penny for the children,
And let it chime a holy music on the plate
Among the others given in the name of God
And His angels in good suits that come among them
To watch the quaint alteration of the Bread and Wine,
And the meat and water given, to their flesh.
Yes, their streets are dry as neglected bones,
And listen to the flies that choir around their sides
Clouding their skipping scraps of flesh that play
At pounds and pennies in the puffing gutters.
In your good, cool suit, come to their rescue;
What will it cost? Not the hundredth of a day
In this their sunny land of your holiday;
There's no deception, look at the children round her door,
They are hers, and they are the truly poor,

That sit in the tourist's sunlight
And watch him from the leaning door.

II

Where the brats crowd at the doors of wombs
Waiting for the masculine care-taker, or husband,
To let them in;
Where the streets are driest, and the cooling winds
Wear mantles of the hardest dust:
See how the little ones play with buttons,
Cigarette stubs, pieces of wall,
That a flying saucer, this a rocket, that the earth,
Spitting on road-rocks for bombs that hiss with heat;
Look at their wells of eyes,
And their mothers', cushioned in leather,
And their fathers', caught in cobwebs of dried expressions.

They have nothing to do, or no money,
And the heat of the light, those are the reasons,
More fun than cinema,
Less thirsty than Sunday outings;
And it is cried aloud by some visitors to the quarter
That this is the best work of man:
To admit, at whatever price, children.

III

And the music is in the eyes as the green trunks weave,
Or in the scent bound there until the hose.
I cannot make stories that music their lives,
Not having the speech they recount themselves in;
I see only that the children come and come
And the dry heat dusts the trees.
Waiters take something in their palm,
And ripe tourists blink in the sun.

7

The Collector

Caught in a fold of living hills he failed,
For, out of his childhood, he had wandered on
An alien soil;
Extending his amiable senses, he found them blind.

The senses still, the reason kept its sway;
Nothing could be of conscious choice but still he chose
Observations made to stir him in default of love.
And thus the beauty and the terror of his life
Moved him mildly. This living landscape where before
He failed, was absorbing, with the horny rocks and the
Mist that glittered like a skin,
And with reasonable curiosity he saw
Crows fall from the sky, lilac tongues
Of death in the square-cut hedge; such omens
Were full of interest.

A busy life it was, watching the people with the
Gay clothes and the lives whipped like tops;
The tongued folk who burned with
The fire that warmed his watching.

At the end, as he would have wished, the Divine
Fingers plucked him from this skin
With much pain for both;
For he was interested in his illness,
And the world, strange to relate, had grown fond of him.

Lazarus and the Sea

The tide of my death came whispering like this
Soiling my body with its tireless voice.
I scented the antique moistures when they sharpened
The air of my room, made the rough wood of my bed, (most
    dear),
Standing out like roots in my tall grave.
They slopped in my mouth and entered my plaited blood
Quietened my jolting breath with a soft argument
Of such measured insistence, untied the great knot of my heart.
They spread like whispered conversations
Through all the numbed rippling tissues radiated
Like a tree for thirty years from the still centre
Of my salt ovum. But this calm dissolution
Came after my agreement to the necessity of it;
Where before it was a storm over red fields
Pocked with the rain and the wheat furrowed
With wind, then it was the drifting of smoke
From a fire of the wood, damp with sweat,
Fallen in the storm.

I could say nothing of where I had been,
But I knew the soil in my limbs and the rain-water
In my mouth, knew the ground as a slow sea unstable
Like clouds and tolerating no organisation such as mine
In its throat of my grave. The knotted roots
Would have entered my nostrils and held me
By the armpits, woven a blanket for my cold body
Dead in the smell of wet earth, and raised me to the sky
For the sun in the slow dance of the seasons.
Many gods like me would be laid in the ground
Dissolve and be formed again in this pure night
Among the blessing of birds and the sifting water.

9

But where was the boatman and his gliding punt?
The judgment and the flames? These happenings
Were much spoken of in my childhood and the legends.
And what judgment tore me to life, uprooted me
Back to my old problems and to the family,
Charged me with unfitness for this holy simplicity?

A Storm

Somebody is throttling that tree
By the way it's threshing about;
I'm glad it's no one I know, or me,
The head thrust back at the throat,

Green hair tumbled and cracking throat.
His thumbs drive into her windpipe,
She cannot cry out,
Only swishing and groaning: death swells ripe,

The light is dimming but the fight goes on.
Chips strike my window. In the morning, there
Stands the tree, still, bushy and calm,
Not as I saw it, twisted heel to ear,

But fluffed up, boughs chafing slightly.
What's become of her attacker?
I'm glad he's not mine or known to me,
Flipped to the ground, heel over ear:

She preens herself, with a soft bough-purr.
Was he swallowed up, lip over ear?
He's gone anyway. The path is thick in her fur.
Am I a friend, may I walk near?

Questions

Questions that I have are put,
And lost in the scuppers of his brain,
His head is nearer the clouds than mine,
Questions that I put are lost.

His eyes are larger, and his hands,
He stalks in rooms and shuts the door,
His voice calls higher from the floor
Than mine, and larger are his hands

And he can mend the broken toy
That in a wilful fit I bust
And gouge its eye because I must,
He puts it together for his boy.

He never shouts and never weeps
Never runs out on the lawn,
Silently puts back the torn,
Was he ever as small as I?

Control

Saws snoring, and the bunches of dust
Puffy under the grease-shined shaft
Are used by men not amateurs, who must
Know how wood goes. A boy I knew calfed
Off a hand on one of those because of a curving knot,

Who loved the way the wood went and how
The saw warmed it, and wanted to speed the rot
Of the blade, and on to the dust sow
Tiny seeds of water with the saw to cool it.
I think it was the idea of decay that fascinated him
And how unlike the other kinds this bit
The way you wanted it. The bound-up rim
Of his stump still sometimes buzzes with recollection.
He was another who knew our destination.

On Catching a Dog-Daisy in the Mower

"Well, that was silly; too near the edge:
  White flesh goes flying and the bee escapes.
  It was an old flower anyway and not a prize,
  Inside, the shade of good tobacco finely-grained.
  What a shock the bee got though, snatching away
  His stool like that as he sat down.
  I'll clear it up; so white a flesh
  Against the green; I'll let it char,
  But tuck the mangled neck back again
  Right out of sight, behind the crowded bush
  Of roses red as—how they shine: it seems to hum."
So I buzzed about my jobs, mumbling my mind,
Stringing sentences and trying words
And soon forgot whose flesh was white, and shreds
Charred back to soil, and what roses were as red as,

12

And summer dry as, now, and how swift
The tawny humming bee snapped away.
"I'd better pick the white bits up,
And put them on the heap, for tidiness."

(*After the death of a close friend in an accidental fall*)

The Bird

That bird upon the birch branch stirs my ear
With a long cool pole of sound,
The spiders shift uneasily behind the bearded boards
Piled damp beside the woodshed,
For it underhunts a tatter of curled bark
And when it cannot get a grub it takes a spider
And does not refuse their bodies in its beak
The black-and-suet bodies that I shudder at
Nor their bitter break of juices at the bite,
And flies worms rot-coated to its children,

But so unlike we please each other
Since I put out water from my drinking tap
And summer and winter it stirs the garden
Out of its hot body with a long cool pole of sound.

Dead Bird

Flies cauterise as they eat dabbing the parts
Making a warped map of our bird
Scab hillocks and the hard brume of weals,
Ochre bars and divots of gristle.
I shovel it off my lawn with a hoe,
I trowel a hole of centipedes and sand
Savages that now stray without thoughts
Through all the upstart galleries of that flier
Whose memory lies in feathers crinkling
Over the whole endeavour of our sun-dried lawn.

Memorial

(David Redgrove: 28th December 1937—24th December 1957)

Two photographs stand on the dresser
Joined up the spine. Put away
They fold until they kiss each other,
But put out, they look across the room.
My brother and myself. He is flushed and pouting
With heart, and standing square,
I, already white-browed and balding,
Float there, it seems, and look away.
You could look at us and say I was the one of air,
And he the brother of earth
Who, in Christmas-time, fell to his death.

Fancy, yes; but if you'd seen him in his life
There'd be his bright blond hair, and that flush,
And the mouth always slightly open, and the strength
Of body: those muscles! swelled up with the hard hand-
    springs at night
Certainly, but strong. I, on the other hand
Was remote, cross, and disengaged, a proper
Bastard to my brother, who enjoyed things,
Until he was able to defend himself. It's June;
Everything's come out in flush and white,
In ruff and sun, and tall green shoots
Hard with their sap. He's ashes
Like this cigarette I smoke into grey dryness.
I notice outside my window a tree of blossom,
Cherries, I think, one branch bending heavy
Into the grey road to its no advantage.
The hard stone scrapes the petals off,
And the dust enters the flower into its peak.
It is so heavy with flowers it bruises itself:
It has tripped, you might say, and fallen,
Cannot get up, so heavy with dust.
The air plays with it, and plays small-chess with the dust.

The Archaeologist

So I take one of those thin plates
And fit it to a knuckled other,
Carefully, for it trembles on the edge of powder,
Restore the jaw and find the fangs their mates.

The thorny tree of which this is the gourd,
Outlasting centuries of grit and water,
Re-engineered by me, stands over there,
Stocky, peeling, crouched and dangling-pawed.

I roll the warm wax within my palm
And to the bone slowly mould a face
Of the jutting-jawed, hang-browed race;
On the brute strength I try to build up a calm,

For it is a woman, by the broad hips;
I give her a smooth skin, and make the mouth mild:
It is aeons since she saw her child
Spinning thin winds of gossamer from his lips.

The Nature of Cold Weather and Other Poems

For No Good Reason

I walk on the waste-ground for no good reason
Except that fallen stones and cracks
Bulging with weed suit my mood
Which is gloomy, irascible, selfish, among the split timbers
Of somebody's home, and the bleached rags of wallpaper.
My trouser-legs pied with water-drops,
I knock a sparkling rain from hemlock-polls,
I crash a puddle up my shin,
Brush a nettle across my hand,
And swear—then sweat from what I said:
Indeed, the sun withdraws as if I stung.

Indeed, she withdrew as if I stung,
And I walk up and down among these canted beams,
    bricks and scraps,
Bitten walls and weed-stuffed gaps
Looking as it would feel now, if I walked back,
Across the carpets of my home, my own home.

Ghosts

The terrace is said to be haunted.
By whom or what nobody knows; someone
Put away under the vines behind dusty glass
And rusty hinges staining the white-framed door
Like a nosebleed, locked; or a death in the pond
In three feet of water, a courageous breath?
It's haunted anyway, so nobody mends it
And the paving lies loose for the ants to crawl through
Weaving and clutching like animated thorns.
We walk on to it,
Like the bold lovers we are, ten years of marriage,
Tempting the ghosts out with our high spirits,
Footsteps doubled by the silence . . .

. . . and start up like ghosts ourselves
Flawed lank and drawn in the greenhouse glass:
She turns from that, and I sit down,
She tosses the dust with the toe of a shoe,
Sits on the pond's parapet and takes a swift look
At her shaking face in the clogged water,
Weeds in her hair; rises quickly and looks at me.
I shrug, and turn my palms out, begin
To feel the damp in my bones as I lever up
And step toward her with my hints of wrinkles,
Crows-feet and shadows. We leave arm in arm
Not a word said. The terrace is haunted,
Like many places with rough mirrors now,
By estrangement, if the daylight's strong.

The Stronghold

We had a fine place to come—
Into the keep of the old oak,
The frill of leaves to challenge through,
The tower-room in the old trunk,
The knot-holes, loops and battlements,
And the chinks wedged open with sunlight,
The fine soft shavings of decay
To putter in, run through our toes.
We were the breathing of the wood,
Its tender core, the faces, watchers, guardians,
Bare and bony-cold in winter,
Warm and odorous in summer
And in the autumn rustling in our leaves.
That is all gone now; by haunting
I learn that oak-tree strongholds are out of fashion
And I grow too big to squeeze inside:
The shadow of my head cuts off the light
And I peer into unrelieved and cramping gloom.
The sun breaks in hiding darting shadows outside
And smooth children's faces form among the rough
    tree-barks.

Two Poems

I. SPRING

To pass by a pondbrink
Trodden by horses

Where among the green horsetails
Even the hoofprints
Shiver with tadpoles
Comma'ed with offspring
And moist buds flick awake
On breeze-floundering sallows.

II. EPHEMERID

The fly is yellowed by the sun,
Her plating heaves, her wings hum,
Her eyes are cobbled like a road,
Her job is done, her eggs are stowed
No matter in what. The sun
Yellows the hemlock she sits upon;
Her death is near, her job is done,
Paddling in pollen and the sun,
She swings upon the white-flowered weed,
As a last duty, yellow with seed,
She falters round the flower-rim,
Falters around the flower-rim.

More Leaves from my Bestiary

I. SPIDER

Now, the spires of a privet fork from the hedge
And stretch a web between them;

The spider-nub eases his grip a trifle, twists a thread safe,
And the afternoon is quiet again.

Damp clouds drift above him; a burst of rain
Runs him back along a vane
To a leaf-shed, while it beads his web
And raises weed-smells from below
Of vetch, fumitory, and small mallow.

Hanging there are a dozen or so
Brown shells which tremble.
The curtain is ripped from the sun, and grass again
Leaps into its fumble:

Ants totter with their medicine balls and cabers, stone walls
Pop with their crickets;
A bluefly, furry as a dog, squares up
To the web and takes it with a jump like a hoop

And spider springs round like a man darting
To the fringes of a dogfight;

Tugging like a frantic sailor, buzzing like a jerky sawyer,
Fly finishes in swaddling
Tight as a knot
From the spinnerets' glistening.

And though spider
Hangs a little lower than the sun
Over all their heads, all
Seem ignorant of that passing;
The afternoon, the ebullience increases
Among the low boughs of the weeds
And spider steady, like a lichened glove
Only a little lower than the sun; none

Takes account of that to and fro passing,
Or of the manner of that death in swaddling.

II. BASILISK

Rising above the fringe of silvering leaves
A finger, tanned and scaly, gorgeous, decayed,
Points to the shivering clouds, then turns down
Most slowly, towards you. The light catches, cold and hard
Pulls round the polished bone of fingernail
Arrests attention, the prey falls dead.

Bone mirrors have the quickest way to die
The sunlight loses strength and sap drained
Out and lost, distils a beam of purest mortality
Set in the velvet sockets of a fabled bird.
A mandarin of birds, exalted, alone
Sweeping its cold avenue of dying trees
Its restlessness oppressed for new fuel, warm
And busy not to lift its eyes, unrealised sin
Committed out of favour, and it dies.

But when it dies the silks collapse and draw aside.
The idle naturalist to draw this legend to its wisest close,
Pries. The walking-stick at first disturbs a swarm
But no danger from the tawny ground, it lies
As still as where it dropped. Newspaper and a spade
A tin tray in the quietest room; probes,
Licks like an eagle with his sharpest knives.
Fat, flesh, yes, and normal bones
Sincerely documented, the head from behind now
The brain, enlarged, hard and crisp as ice
No poison, the smell of preservatives, the face

At last, nostrils and beak, a wrinkled neck,
The eyelids closed. He pulls these aside,
They rustle, a smell like pungent spice

He catches. How curious, the eyes as dead
And white as buttons, hard, adamantine, he tries
To scratch them with his knife, with no effect,
Revolves the problem in his clouding head.
Then the light catches, and he dies.

More Voices

I. GRAVID MOTHER AND CRIPPLE

White pyramid on grey
trundles askew
at the side of my eye;
she comes forward
bloused and skirted,
her rib-cage limps
on grey hips below,
proper creases
vomit bunches
spasm, recover
the tail works free;
bent-axled
she rolls across me.

A pestle grinding in granite mortar some birds choked,
As an axe rings to the wood they sang,

Others like the flutes of the bubbling stream
Gushed life at their silent partners.

She eases down on a bench
With a fine twig she strokes the water,
From the pervasive and wailing treble
Like an ear-knuckling crowd fish flee;
She looks, I look away;
She looks into my womb,
And she pities me.

II. IN THE BUSH

One beast unknown breaks its bundle of dry sticks,
Another thumps its way upstairs, a third pulls a zip,
And in a bush one calls from such loneliness of heart
That makes my heart start, turn and lean
Towards the bush, the dry sticks and the stones.
The hunter shifts his rifle on his lap:
"What a moon! Like a polished silver bowl;
It shines with brightness. This fire
Will want a bit of seeing to . . ." indeed it did
If the moon was not to overwhelm us all
And make a light so one could see like day
Except for shadow-rivers from the slenderest sticks
So that the beasts too could slink in safety
And push such calls up against the late hour
As human hearts of loneliness'd turn aside
In the shadows to meet up with fangs.
No, we had to be certain of the time of day
(Night's night, and dangerous), and exist
In the trembling orange light of burning sticks.

III. OUT OF REACH

Heather rusts dry on the hot brow of the cliff—
The crested waves skip into the bay
Like small birds flocking, claws flicking;
Nearby, two inches from my eye,
A caterpillar bows a green grass-stem
And my eye fumbles with its padded links or at once
Sweeps down and up the gorge. It's hot;
The land stands paddling in its sweat;
And my sweat dries firm. With the cliff solid
And the sun solid on my back I am on my own
And the wind presses me back, but all around
Is sheer evidence of the suicide of the land:
Sliced gorges spouting brine. I'm all right

(Except by poring bushes at the very brink
Of blackberries, that trip the tongue
On cobbled tartness bounding down
Or syrups seeping into space.)

IV. THE SOLITUDE

Heavy, holy faces throng the house,
Swearing agony from the ceiling, agonised remorse
Sweeps over the ceiling—high in the moulding
The spider cracks his web through yellow eyeballs;
Curtain-folds gust quiet laughter.

Wriggling in the steam of my breakfast-coffee
Are refusal, righteousness, misery of charity;
Stains of half a moan sadden a whole ceiling;
My own in the mirror the only sane one among them,
The rockery outside knuckles my mouth in prayer.

The doorbell. I hitch my trouser-legs in pleated smiles
And request my visitor to be seated.

V. COURTSHIP

I like to look a man straight in the eye
And know what he is thinking, I can see
He's good or bad, and act accordingly.
We'll draw the curtains on the beating windows
Blinking with light rain, blossom, birds in twos,
And turn the sofa with our backs across it,
Opening the TV window for an hour or two.
It stands there like an acquaintance with a single eye
Bright, transparent; looking through
I see the clever, beating mind within—
On the sofa, holding hands with you.

VI. THE HOST

I sulk. I am tense and swollen. I will recover.
Veins like roots corrode my skull.
I champ grits from my enamel.
The angle of my mouth is cracked from bellowing.

I am bastinadoed from my stamping.
But I shall get over it, though I squat shuddering,
Elbows drilling knees. I hold my eyes
Clenched in their flesh, and a mouth
Packed with saliva. Ah!

I am myself again. They have brought fresh straw!
To crisp my steps as I advance, talons outstretched,
    nictitating,
To greet my pink visitors through the mild steel bars.

Malagueño

Warming his buttocks on the hot stone at his master's threshold
He flaps his eyelids against the light; from his shoulder
Brushes the dust; the poor in this country are rarely cold.
His trousers stiffen in the heat, as starched, and moulder,
His sweat ferments. He is a simple labourer with a daily wage
Sawing up sewer pipes in the direct sun, or dragging them
Along trenches muddy with man-sweat. There is no cage
He bruises his hands against. His offspring teem
Under a thatch of rushes near the sea-front.

He can mount
Under the guidance of the church until his eyes glow like a
    saint's;
He can have another child; for sixpence he can get drunk
And be a torero, the government, or a saint; he has no taints
On his soul that the church refuses, he is not sunk
Even by adultery, just as in the streets, hot to his rope-soled feet,
Tobacco-juice or dung whitens with light like warm milk from
    the pitch-dark teat.

Two Elegies

I. VARIATION ON LORCA

Neither the house nor the rooms
Nor the ants under the stones, nor the horses,
Nor our child nor the misty evenings
Knows you. You are dead.

The headstones, the white satin
Into which you crumble,
My memory of you, know nothing
Of where you are. You are dead.

Autumn will come with its snails creeping,
Apples blushing,
Boughs pushing through the rent bushes but
None of us wants to be with you now;
We are ignorant and frightened;
No one would wish to look into your eyes. You
   are dead.

You are dead, piled with the rest of earth's dead,
The smoked ends of earth's dead;
Nobody knows you from them, or wants to know
The condition into which your body has fallen,
But I sing,
Standing for your posterity, of your restlessness,
Your profile, the purity of your understanding,
Your appetite for hazard and the taste of death,
Of the sorrow in recollection of your gaiety.

I doubt whether we shall soon see another,
So evident a man, so rich in adventure;

I sing in words that moan and raise
A sad breeze among all that knew you.

That last full-stop dries like a bright eye closing.

II. THE IDIOT

He dreams under the brown hair of the blouse-button shim-
    mering with breath
His rose mouth fills with dew and his fingers twitch.
There is no time beyond his fourteen years
When the white muscle of the dug does not fill and bloom
In the clear unwrinkled viscera of his head.

Men beget men, and the angels of chance experiment,
And he looks through eyes that catch no portion of their
    glory.
What kicking lark in the belly tore the thin sheet of his brain
And let it burgeon like the pink-gilled fungus and feed
Like the flowerless fungus or feed
Like the soft mussel in its chalky shell? He cannot cry for
    water
And waits with gaping shell for the soft tide of his mother.

I escape out of doors into the wood
Where the brown-hatted fungus burgeons under the tree-
    shade;
I pass where the bracken stirs over the crushed sticks of its
    kind . . .

. . . and over my bed
The dawn fills the curved sky and freshens
The tight cheeks of the early farmer who spits
Into the pash of dead leaves. Now
The bright globe loses its animal heat
Becoming cold as the dew that fell in cold, born to death.

The Ghostly Father

He'd had enough of lying in the furze.
He combed gnats out of his beard,
Shrugged tendrils off his habit.

He'd try the road. But Goodness!
He was hungry. He wrung
The hem of his robe and sipped dew.

His bare feet had worn through. Thorns shivered
     on them,
They sank in the pasture and rattled flints
As he padded to the blot of a distant town.

He knew his face was seamed with pollen
     and earth,
But, peering over a smooth puddle,
Saw only the moon, blown to the full.

The trees enrolled him overhead.
A religious should not jump at shadows.
He rattled his rosary. A traveller glimpsing,
     ran.

This was discouraging. He sought the ditch
And burrowed through turf and fetched against
     bed-rock:
He would not walk, but lay blinking on packed
     roots;
Perhaps one day men would be more spiritual.

Our Friend

(Or, The Trouble with Harry)

When we found ourselves with no cart that day
To carry our friend in
Or even a plank for a stretcher, or a trunk as a dray,
We just let him stiffen

And we waited for hours that way
For who would carry his dead friend like a lover,
Hoisting him like a roll of blanket? He lay
Reproaching us for hours, I say.

Well, after the sun had gone, we saw ourselves
By the glimmer of his face, as it were;
And we laid him out, composed not as we'd like to
    appear,
And he set that way.

I fear it will be awkward for the coffin.
We brought him back like a walking table, or a stag-
    gering crab;
My shoulder's blistered with his heel. What he'll lie in
I don't know. As he's drab

Already in a good stiff serge, that might do,
Or you could borrow a wide wardrobe. Not a few
Would approve that idea; but save the mirror. And for
    Goodness' sake,
In this climate, spare a second wake.

We came by moonlight, and cooled our feet in the
    lake.

Expectant Father

Final things walk home with me through Chiswick Park,
Too much death, disaster; this year
All the children play at cripples
And cough along with one foot in the gutter.
But now my staircase is a way to bed
And not the weary gulf she sprinted down for doorbells
So far gone on with the child a-thump inside;
A buffet through the air from the kitchen door that sticks
Awakes a thumb-size fly. Butting the rebutting window-pane
It shouts its buzz, so I fling the glass up, let it fly
Remembering as it skims to trees, too late to swat,
That flies are polio-whiskered to the brows
With breeding-muck, and home
On one per cent of everybody's children.

So it is the week when Matron curfews, with her cuffs,
And I draw back. My wife, round as a bell in bed, is white
    and happy.
Left to myself I undress for the night
By the fine bright wires of lamps: hot tips
To burrowing cables, the bloodscheme of the house,
Where flame sleeps. That,
With a shallow on the mattress from last night,
Is enough to set me thinking on fired bones
And body-prints in the charcoal of a house, how
Darkness stands for death, and how afraid of sleep I am;
And fearing thus, thus I fall fast asleep.

But at six o'clock, the phone rings in—success!
The Sister tells me our son came up with the sun:
It's a joke she's pleased to make, and so am I.

I see out of the window it's about a quarter high,
And ·promises another glorious day.

The Nature of Cold Weather

FIRST GRACE

Chills and pain, oh; now we'll have to keep
The house very warm, and the snowface
From snubbing itself up against the panes,
And lip-grease to face the winds in front of April.
Naturally we go out; but for pleasure?
One last walk to watch the red leaves frosting,
And then we draw a curtain on the floured-up window.

Although, with lip-grease, and great husky clothes,
Looking for life along the banks of rivers,
I sometimes give thanks for beauty of all seasons,
Creaking for pleasure through the snow.

I

The moon stares for an instant, then a cloud lays
Flat on her mouth like a finger;
Over the acres of ground-leaves,
The spiking darts that were trees,
Again she steals upon them with her red.

II

Like a copper bowl burning before a fire,
She's red, and rouges the soused leaves

That take a mere street light and shoot it back in
   beams,
Or overcrust quietly in the colder dark.

The houses stuffed with light
Rest back on their oars of light
Over the dark flowing of the street.

III

Among this catalogue of crusts and copper,
Light pointers through chinks, *droplets*
Beaten wide on a cold anvil, and red-bayed clouds,
We walk breaking the beams.
Blowing through gloves, and freshly hobbled from
   a loose drain,
Cursing the young builders,
We know through our shoes that the winter has
   come
Cracking like glass. Good God!—
Now the air is stuffed with feathers and we walk
   on wool,
The barking radios tethered to their territories,
And silence grows nicely, balanced on a falling flake;
So we hurry home, before our tempers break.

IV

When we have come to our door, finally,
Warm food and my wife pack me up in sleep;
And do I dream of brisked fur nibbling at the skin,
Fledglings frozen like cracking lips,

How the birds keep warm with cheep and chime?
Not these, but scenic crusts and copper,
Crisp crystals and their shooting beams
As the moon passes over the extinguished street.

V

Somewhere the ice-spirits must creep
Gently scratching through the copper bowl,
Or sprawling enormously through the snow
Pinned down in pleasure of the slickering white:
To know whom is to burn at mind and hand,
Or round the cold-shocked temples grip like iron
Freezing like fledglings that run with thin cracks
Calling aloud on things they could not name:
Not even the hail, beating cold iron of the ground,
Embargo of granaries of seed between the beaks—
So I rest, and am thankful.

VI

The low trees once more rove over the high floors
As if a cursing chimney-sweep wept with out-
    stretched palms
A soft shroud filled with crusty water and with grain;
As grotesque they dangle as if skeletons
Were buried drum-skin-topside down
In the soft drifts of their fallen flesh
Ankles asking for the air. O, absurd
To see those straight bleached planes, those discs,
Those carefully-moulded hunchbacks of the wind,
Those steeled streams, and that harping, spidery frost
Quilting the stuffed-out, olive nooks of the weeds,
The beer-head hemlock and the suds of leaves,

And flanks of foliage panting the warm air
All crammed into a seed by weight of cold,
Acres under the husk, and on the husk blank acres.
I feel the coil uncurl and riffle through the flakes,
I see the dormant hedgehogs with their eggs
Kept under blood beneath the tatter tapping
Of the broken blackthorn at their eaves.

VII

And the white is a snow-plate,
And the pupil a hail-knot,
The arms folded fur.

VIII

Runt-head of wood-trunk bulging with snow,
With knots popped away;
With the white of a snow-disc,
And the stare of an ice-stone
Insolent of warmth:
My new overcoat and my woollen, unwooden
    warmth.

IX

And my fist that strikes it
Cracks in a leaf-net.
Pain as if crushed
Leases the nail-quicks.
Hands are packed back into gloves
(Great clumsy white hands)
Wet with the misery
Of the smoothing-out of streams.

X

O, stop it; it's just water, isn't it?
White as good linen
                    That scars the patient.
Very beautiful, I think. The soft flurries
And crystalline formations
                    That cut like glass.
Well, I'm glad I'm not out in it.
A good book, food, and fire
                    When the white radiation
                    Sinks into living skin like the fire.

XI

And the carefully-shaded bough, blackly-bellied,
That slinks across the snow half-undetected;
The half-trees,
And the sky with its half-solid winds and no horizon
And deeper white outstanding on the white around;
I stand with my shadow on my head
At the centre of a white globe
(Built up, and, oh, all built upon,
Soft so that heels and scalp grow mixed together,)
Creaking cold-shucked to the warm banks of the
    river
Where red weed waves on black bog still.

XII

As one slow ache, out in the windy snow,
Time to observe a few things *as the flesh*
Squeezes pain downwards, bleaching skin into my heart,
My innermost things, underground.

37

Two ponds of blank grey ice with grizzled reeds,
A heaped-up chine with two dark rabbit-holes,
A slash of almost-frozen stream with meeting teeth,
Clashing and tinkling, with brisk beard tugging at its
  banks,
A col of thumbed snow in billowed rests,
A swelling upland beating with black shrubs,
White muscles, declivities, skews and runnels,
A follicle that the wind reached in and coiled,
A sloping valley with one creaking tree,
An extinct stream and a fork-tailed ridge;
In the distance a range of ten mist foot-hills,
And overall the bleached and dangling sky.

XIII

I blink my crusting eyes one second. There's the sky;
Here is the centre of a white-quilted globe.
Sight dabs at the ice-rims of my lids: they will not close;
Sight is beneath the ice like fish or stones.
It stares round the heap of nose at melting teeth,
At my melting, clashing teeth,
My flurrying chest whiting-out the shrubs,
The deep cutting on my runted genitals.
I need to stir my legs but they are extinct,
Wind overturns the hills, and as I sob
Ice gun-cracks on my ponds and I am blind.

XIV

Quickly the ponds freeze over once again;
See, there is the floor of me, my things
Lying around, my whiteness and my softness and my flurry
Now at the centre of a dazzling globe.

The wind turns my head in manes. By a bevelled ridge
There is a hand of branching, snow-topped streets.
I feel the small shoots gyrate and prick
As they cast crusts upward through my knees,
And all the people have their fires at my nails.

XV

O, what beauty in the ice-rose,
The heels and skews,
The bevels, ramps and biases of snows,
The glass thorns, the grey flat eyes.

XVI

And I shall close my teeth
On the chugging stream, and with my growth
Balanced like silence on the snow-flake,
Smoothe the world in white-sleep, with its branch and
   ache.

XVII

The fires stir and flush their brick and grounds—

Breathe the solid wind, heap high mounds:
Make all right!
Make all white!

XVIII

The breakup of the giant . . .
First the houses burn his fingers

Flushing up brown soil along his arms,
His whiteness smutches, and the pricking comes
    intense,
Freckles and patches, wens and mud-craters
Where those beautiful declivities shone,
And long before, his eyes broke, and he is blind . . .

XIX

His teeth unclench and jaw tumbles
Cheeks sink flat in jagged thaws
Like the cracking of fledglings or of hands,
And black branching cracks grow green and pimpled,
And grass, not pleasure, skrimp-pins him to the ground.
His withered limbs lie as short-ice in the grass,
In ice-weals along the shaded bumps
Drawn after his teeth and jaws, legs and lion-like head,
Brain, spirit and crystalline reflection
Along the chugging streams
That feed on him and grow plush along their sides.
The sun shines on the green meadows,
The chines and valleys, tufts and hillocks
Quilted with daisies and with buttercups,
Misty with gossamer and pollen,
And his heels drum in the stream
As the playing children come.

LAST GRACE

Now he is not dead by any means,
But just upon us all again;

40

We are glad to be indoors;
His spirit always tends to shiver round the corners,
Blow off the sea, creep on us at night-time,
And often the door wakes us with his colours,
White feathers and a sleety wind,
Tiring my wife and me more than ever
As he lays his siege along our husky flanks.
But we'd not be the immortal snow with his quietist fever,
And losing war (for we fight no more);
For which we give our thanks.

Spider-Boy

Nearly tea-time, and as the clock-hands fall
The small boy tires of thumping with his ball
The spider, sunning, studies from the wall.

He reaches for the interesting crack
Stuffed with blue veils. She dances on her rack

Of mincing shins behind her farthest silk
Where the studded egg-ball hangs. He, scarcely off
  his milk,

Follows worming with an ear-finger. She, in fits
From the reech, the whorls, the balls of sweat, the pits,

Swings up and wires her belly to the brood-loaf,
Dragging deep folds fanning to the roof;

The webbing swells and snaps
But rocking she holds fast with her tight body-straps

And he hauls off blurred with rags before the worst,
Leaving the door clear and slithering with dust.

She clambers down and waits. She knows
Shaggy timbers come with pounding blows

And ragged steel screeches on brick to burst
Grape-weights of spinners bloodying their silk first

Then back to slive the eggs. He pulls up a sock,
Peers through the bombed space to the steeple-clock.

Not teatime quite—he can get back if he's quick.
He unclasps his knife and whets it on a brick.

At the Edge of the Wood

First, boys out of school went out of their way home
To detonate the windows; at each smash
Piping with delight and skipping for fright
Of a ghost of the old man popping over his hedge,
Shrieking and nodding from the gate.
Then the game palled, since it was only breaking the
   silence.
The rain sluiced through the starred gaps,
Crept up walls and into the brick; frost bit and
   munched;

Weeds craned in and leant on the doors.
Now it is a plot without trees let into the wood
Piled high with tangle and tousle
Buried parapets and roots picking at the last mortar
Though the chimney still stands sheathed in leaves
And you can see for the time being where in a nook
A briony burst its pot with a shower of roots
And back through the press of shrubs and stems
Deep-coils into the woods.

Mists

They do not need the moon for ghostliness
These mists jostling the boles,
These boy-wraiths and ogre-fumes
That hollow to a breasting walk;
They are harmless enough in all conscience,
Wetting eyelashes and growing moulds,
And do not speak at all, unless their walking flood
Is a kind of languid speech. Like ghosts
Dawn filches them for dews.
They wink at me from grasses pushed aside
And impart a high polish to my shoes
That dry in dullness, milky, sloven leather,
From walking in ghostways where tall mists grope.

Mr Waterman

"*Now, we're quite private in here. You can tell me your troubles. The pond, I think you said . . .*"

"We never really liked that pond in the garden. At times it was choked with a sort of weed, which, if you pulled one thread, gleefully unravelled until you had an empty basin before you and the whole of the pond in a soaking heap at your side. Then at other times it was as clear as gin, and lay in the grass staring upwards. If you came anywhere near, the gaze shifted sideways, and it was you that was being stared at, not the empty sky. If you were so bold as to come right up to the edge, swaggering and talking loudly to show you were not afraid, it presented you with so perfect a reflection that you stayed there spellbound and nearly missed dinner getting to know yourself. It had hypnotic powers."

"*Very well. Then what happened?*"

"Near the pond was a small bell hung on a bracket, which the milkman used to ring as he went out to tell us upstairs in the bedroom that we could go down and make the early-morning tea. This bell was near a little avenue of rose-trees. One morning, very early indeed, it tinged loudly and when I looked out I saw that the empty bottles we had put out the night before were full of bright green pondwater. I had to go down and empty them before the milkman arrived. This was only the beginning. One evening I was astounded to find a brace of starfish coupling on the ornamental stone step of the pool, and, looking up, my cry to my wife to come and look was stifled by the sight of a light peppering of barnacles on the stems of the rose-trees. The vermin had evidently crept there, taking advantage of the thin film of moisture on the ground after the recent very wet weather. I dipped a finger into the pond and tasted it: it was brackish."

"*But it got worse.*"

"It got worse: one night of howling wind and tempestuous rain I heard muffled voices outside shouting in rural tones: 'Belay

44

there, you lubbers!' 'Box the foresail capstan!' 'A line! A line! Give me a line there, for Davy Jones' sake!' and a great creaking of timbers. In the morning, there was the garden-seat, which was too big to float, dragged tilting into the pond, half in and half out."

"But you could put up with all this. How did the change come about?"

"It was getting playful, obviously, and inventive, if ill-informed, and might have got dangerous. I decided to treat it with the consideration and dignity which it would probably later have insisted on, and I invited it in as a lodger, bedding it up in the old bathroom. At first I thought I would have to run canvas troughs up the stairs so it could get to its room without soaking the carpet, and I removed the flap from the letter-box so it would be free to come and go, but it soon learnt to keep its form quite well, and get about in macintosh and goloshes, opening doors with gloved fingers."

"Until a week ago . . ."

"A week ago it started sitting with us in the lounge (and the electric fire had to be turned off, as the windows kept on steaming up). It had accidentally included a goldfish in its body, and when the goggling dolt swam up the neck into the crystal-clear head, it dipped its hand in and fumbled about with many ripples and grimaces, plucked it out, and offered the fish to my wife, with a polite nod. She was just about to go into the kitchen and cook the supper, but I explained quickly that goldfish were bitter to eat, and he put it back. However, I was going to give him a big plate of ice-cubes, which he would have popped into his head and enjoyed sucking, although his real tipple is distilled water, while we watched television, but he didn't seem to want anything. I suppose he thinks he's big enough already."

"Free board and lodging, eh?"

"I don't know what rent to charge him. I thought I might ask him to join the river for a spell and bring us back some of the money that abounds there: purses lost overboard from pleasure-steamers, rotting away in the mud, and so forth. But he has grown very intolerant of dirt, and might find it difficult to get clean again. Even worse, he might not be able to free himself from his rough dirty cousins, and come roaring back as an impossible green seething giant, tall as the river upended, buckling into the sky, and swamp us and the whole village as well. I shudder to think what would happen if he got as far as the sea, his spiritual home: the country would be in danger. I am at my wits' end, for he is idle, and lounges about all day."

"*Well, that's harmless enough . . .*"

"If he's not lounging, he toys with his shape, restlessly. Stripping off his waterproof, he is a charming dolls'-house of glass, with doors and windows opening and shutting; a tree that thrusts up and fills the room; a terrifying shark-shape that darts about between the legs of the furniture, or lurks in the shadows of the room, gleaming in the light of the television-tube; a fountain that blooms without spilling a drop; or, and this image constantly recurs, a very small man with a very large head and streaming eyes, who gazes mournfully up at my wife (she takes no notice), and collapses suddenly into his tears with a sob and a gulp. Domestic, pastoral-phallic, maritime-ghastly, stately-gracious or grotesque-pathetic: he rings the changes on a gamut of moods, showing off, while I have to sit aside slumped in my armchair unable to compete, reflecting what feats he may be able to accomplish in due course with his body, what titillating shapes impose, what exaggerated parts deploy, under his macintosh. I dread the time (for it will come) when I shall arrive home unexpectedly early, and hear a sudden scuffle-away in the waste-pipes, and find my wife ('just out of the shower, dear') with that moist look in her eyes, drying her hair: and then to hear him swaggering in from the garden drains, talking loudly about his day's excursion, as if nothing at all had been going on. For he learns greater charm each day, this Mr Waterman, and can be as stubborn as winter and gentle as the warm rains of spring."

"*I should say that you have a real problem there, but it's too early for a solution yet, until I know you better. Go away, take a week off from the office, spend your time with your wife, relax, eat plenty of nourishing meals, plenty of sex and sleep. Then come and see me again. Good afternoon.*

"The next patient, nurse. Ah, Mr Waterman. Sit down, please. Does the gas fire trouble you? No? I can turn it off if you wish. Well now, we're quite private in here. You can tell me your troubles. A married, air-breathing woman, I think you said. . . ."

At the White Monument and Other Poems

A Silent Man

I love the cold; it agrees with me,
I am minded like its petrifaction,
Or do I mean perfection? My heart
Is cold and loves to stroll through cold,
And seems to see a better speech
Rolling in fat clouds of breath.
I keep talk for my walks, silent clouds
That flow in ample, mouthing white
Along the paths. At home
Where I've closeted my wife
And instituted children in the warm
I keep my silence, lest
Those I love, regard, catch cold from me
As though I strolled through mould, and breathing,
Puffed white clouds to spore more fur.
I never take them on my long cold walks alone,
I save them for a warmer time, some kind of spring;
Saved up in me like frozen seeds among
Crisp-flaring turf, stiff marsh, gagged stream,
Paths the skidding ferrule will not prick;
Where floes creak and yearn at floes
To fuse and bind the Thames for walking on.

This narrowing path punctuated with my stick,
This fuming field where in galoshes
I can watch winter tinkle in the stream

And clap its ice across the water-voice
Where it buttocks through the marsh,

And throttle birds, or shoo them south,
Crazing its flat glum sky with trees . . .

And leaves waggled till they snap and drop,
The robin crouching on his back

Fur-legged amid the bristling white,
Horned twig, fence fanged, whetted blades . . .

Fur them of its own even colour
To cling and blur and sheet,

These are my walks;
Where winter acts and silences,

Where all is firming underfoot,
Where I can watch the cold flat water

Fizz into my prints
Till I can shatter crusts; my walks.

Lake Now-and-Again

A bird cried out like a cracking stick; I blushed and pulled up my trousers. . . .

We had passed an empty cottage with a window open on a neatly turned-down bed and a quiet and dusty grandfather clock . . .

And afterwards we felt that the sounds of our romp had reached the smarmy ears of the worms cramped like white knitting in the under-turf caves—they knew—the bird that snapped out at us as we were getting up knew—so did the skeletons flouncing up to the dark altars in the drowned cathedral deep in the lake whose banks shook at our vehemence . . .

And if the blue sky-gods knew they would stoop down suddenly and sip up all the water in a great whirling funnel to expose us, the skeletons collapsed in the ooze, peering up sagely through the tiny lakes of blue water caught in their eye-sockets, the knowing worms looping away into the mud, skulls piled like rocks, our secret place filled with a sudden silent audience . . .

And we ran, still gripping hands . . .

And there was a little carriage empty and quiet in the lane, the travellers gone off to set up a lakeside fete—their horses respectful enough, jingling the harness mildly now and then—gone to rehearse the band—bang and pipe—(and the lake suddenly flies up to the sky, leaving cliffs and a towering weedy lump in the middle which was a cathedral, water gushing out of the sides and the great rotted west door bursting open mingled with candlesticks and long bones, our parents—proud helpers!—and the mayor himself staring down into the glossy recesses—the comedians striking up with satirical music: they would nod at each other, knowing who was responsible—and jingle back in conference . . .)

. . . still running . . . down the hill we went, out of the wood, pretending they were pounding after us to make us marry, all of them, the gallop of heel-bones, laughter like smashed dishes, sacramental goblets fast-rusted to chest-bones—pretending till panic took us and we ran like maniacs, scattered pebbles and twigs snapping up at our ankles . . .

. . . out of the trees into the open lane where the sky bore down on us with a blue world-wide stare . . .

But it was sleepy with lids of rain, and we got away scot-free while the lake filled up and pressed down, was made good—ourselves back at our two homes eloquently excusing our absence, refreshed, drenched and free—until the next time, in a new place.

The Face
(His Idiot Son)

I. AT DUSK

Veins break upon the clouds, and the sky's clotted face
Shot with freckles, folds on the sun as you
Would bite on a plum and let the juice run down.

More power to your head and hands is my toast
As I swallow my own head in my cups
In full control of my lips and their juices,
You with your red bib of a tongue,
It is high enjoyment to write of you in wine.

II. AT DAWN

I was up early to watch the sun.

Among the clouds massed like a pillow
His face is sleeping. For hair
The sun is spreading blond light on the pillow.
And the cheeks flush, and the strong white
Neck-pillars stir and he looks round, and down,
Blue eyes peeping and lips parting to the morning—

Lips parting till the jaw drops and blows away

And his blue stare will be the sky today.

At the White Monument

(An Interview)

All at once they were talking together,
The one at his best to be kindly as possible,
Explaining that no salary didn't mean he could stay on;
The other wagging his great moon-pate
All tanned like a moon in its coppery rising,
And his eyes white as eggs flashing and flashing,
But never blinking...

And what was the grain of his mahogany?
Laughter? Tears? Mostly shouts, and screams. And more,
He said, waving his hand back to the tall trees
Where the White Monument reared on the warmer glistening
Of heavy roses and warm shaved lawn.
The other snuffed the wholesome green
Oxygen of the cut grass gladly,
And wondered why his eyes wouldn't shut, and could he never
    get
The smoke out of his nostrils, now,

And whether it was a dream that he had, in his nasty
Nest of towels crouched in the pleached spikes of the brush
At the foot of the White Monument. It was certainly a story,
But was it an explanation? And how it refreshed
The commonplace municipal lawns that something of this kind
Might just be tucked away, though it was impossible
And he had his job to do.

It started like a rambling story, his great house,
And how he frightened nobody, because his tan

Blended among the trees, so he could stay. And the miles
Of his house that was, nourishing townships,
The voyages made for it, staff thronged in it,
Families that thrived in its service.

And how they left it as the dreadful boom
Grew in the wind-battering forest of chimneys
That broke the prosperity, he said,
Dropping to his heels, the other reclining, sceptical.
The surge of this surf-sound that broke us;
Men and maids, under-burgesses and stewards
Struck out for themselves on superfluous prosperity
Leaving us empty. With no people
We could not prosper. The booming crash
Tolled out of phase with the blood and shivered the bones,
In the emptying house boomed louder and greater
Through the closets and ballrooms. We kept a few rooms,
And later we slept, by exhaustion, by piling
Act upon act of love.

The one main chimney held sway over us
With its gruff shudder (on the quiet lawn
A breeze blew up and ruffled the grass
Beyond the two men). The sound
Of the hundreds bore in on the one
And scruffed and exhausted, drowned in a lake
Of clear and slowly-shaking sound. It shattered our glass,
It opened our flowers and scattered the petals,
Bruised meat tender as bread, floor deep in a dust-mist
Of generations of wool, cotton, skin-scale and salt.
We lived our sound-sick days and talked
With dry slates and pencil.

He sprang up and walked briskly away,
Turned suddenly and came bowling back—
Here was the clown, the brown bladder-head
Bobbing the spray-white eyes:
My answer was concrete in corpse-heavy sacks,
I hoisted and toiled them up to the roof,
And a cable noosed to the stack on the tractor
Heave-ho and a crash and a great open throb
As if we'd laid the heart bare.

Trotted out a small circle, shambling spoke:
The mixer jarring and churning, shoulder to it,
Grey magma spewed and lolloped down the gap
That to my jarred eyes widened and puckered
In the power of its shout! Up an octave on the first load!
(Great dignity here—ramrod back) throb to a gabble
To a moan, to a shriek, to a whistle,
Up to silence as the pebbly surface
Rose now into light, popped and hiccupped.

Now all was quiet, and I leaned on my spade
Shaking with laughter. A shoulder of ivy
Slipped with a swish. Many tiles protruded
And showed their red hindparts.
A thick pillar of hard breccia now spitted my house,
Bore it up, silenced it.

Quite silent now around, in the park, and tall shadows touched
Heads to low boughs. A little he mimicked
The way he scrambled down the ladders, and flung the front
    door,
And the sprint down the hall to his wife's door
Which stuck a little to his jerk open
On a blank stone wall.

Stone it was, certainly, with a hinged door to it,
Rough, sweating and cool, and a garland of flowers,
Intaglio on the porous stone, looped, repeating the door's
    design,
As though impressed there. Impressed? Yes, now he was right,
And it was stern and sturdy, never to die,
Eighty feet tall with roots of cellarage, his great
Shaft with its weight had leant on the room, and entered.
Pressed, and smoothed down,
As if the shingle had become the tide.

He shuffled and skipped as the beam of heat hit his back,
And skipped out of the way of the puff and crackle underfoot,
As he told how wet slag sparked the power, and his hair puffed
    out in a flash,
Past a coxcomb of flames from the old kitchen range
Weltering and glittering in its lead, and since
He has never lost the smoke in his nostrils.

Up in the nurseries mullions split with the crash of the stones
Falling, and the pit of the foundations filled
Banked and hearthed, with the gush of the mains
Blowing it up to a dazzling light that flowed
From the ragged shell, like a miracle of the Grail,
And the smoke's underbelly like a travelling shoal
Of leaping blood-red dolphins. Then it fell
Not with bellowing and uncouth, but a sound like applause.

He bowed to the applause, then stood to finish,
Arms stretched and spoke without moving:
The flames had fired it clean of the house,
The chimney wrapped round in crimson bellowing,
And the mould of the room at its foot
Began to glow too. Fierce white light

Up out of the pit stretched their shadow across
The lawn crisp as burnt toast, a shadow which thinned
As the tomb looped with its garlands took all the more
Light into itself, with shapes in the dusky stone.
Now it glowed like a jelly and the high back of her chair
Shaped itself through the ruby, and the sight of her shape
Fell through that back.

Then his tan grew on his face as he sidled round, staring,
His lips off his gums and face hardening like fired clay,
And there, as in limelight, her face brightened to sight,
Grew dazzling, of texture of tangled silver wire,
And the lashes of her open eyes that were first deep in shadow
Then shone like blown coals. The little blue flames
Flicked in his clothes, his tears boiled on his cheeks,
His lids fastened up like stone.

Rain fell in a mass. The two facing
Plunged in its downward river and the vision faded
As the stone cooled, with the last the snapping out
Of the two eyes as though they had suddenly winked shut,
Though the figure swum and swung on
Like a drowned person in his eyes.

Beyond, in the pit of the foundations, the stone rattled and
    boomed
While it powdered to good soil in the wet, but neither
Split nor crumbled her monument, but annealed and glazed it
For ever. Half a century trimmed the walks,
Pleached the roses and diverted streams
In the white shadow of the inspiration of this cenotaph
Roasting sparrows and feeding on berries, while soon
All the louts of the town will pull down the trellises heavy with
    roses,

Root up the bushes reeking of verbena, pile them round, the
   whole garden,
And the gas will flame again the heart of her sun
And he run through the flames to her and pass
Into the wall with a puff like thick powder
Only the shadow left, running, with arms outstretched.

Stopped, and the reclining man shuffled uneasily
When he said he would kill to keep the job.

Three Office-Pieces

I. LANTERN

Her fingers go on typing, very lightly,
The office chatters in her teeth and tongue,
Bitter wars despise a cardigan
Over the multiplication tables of the letters.

Come lunchtime, there are sandwiches,
Portly pigeons tottering through the square,
More tut-tuttings about wools, I suppose I
Come up as the boy-friend, remote and cool.

For I am the boy-friend; in my hand
Her fingers go on typing, very lightly,
And though I woo her, often it strikes me cold
I woo myself to love her office chatter.

As why should I not: her swaying figure
Flusters in my mind, as in a lantern,

Throwing itself like light on other women,
Trees, gulls, houses, children,
Revealing itself like light on my profession . . .

But tittle-tattle through my head
Still twiddles like a pop-tune.

II. TELEDREAMY

The weather is television weather, gusty
From the pasty square of light, whirls showering black;
Her fingers go on typing, very lightly.

We wring our eyes in a deluge of shadows—
Snow squalls across the screen—at this
Her father's fingers wriggle in their stains,
Resume their quiet flicker.

I yawn, and shadows run in my mouth, crawl up my nose;
Her mother's jigsaw mouth grins and mourns, grins and mourns,
Though her eyes never leave the story,
Then hailstones gallop up the screen
And her parents disappear in dust
Of whirling shadows, emerge,
Resume their quiet flicker.

Mouth brimming with shadows,
I yawn into our quiet flicker;
We advance, retire; advance, retire
In our quiet flicker.

III. REMINISCENCE

Our wives are harmless since those hunting days
Since confetti broke on the married napes

Birding it into pockets. Now the night
Tames the pale breathers.

                    Talk to me of those early days.
Remember our bodies like the turnlight fishes
Knotting temperatures on white linen palettes,
Floating and listening to the running patter
Of rain on our darkened windows.

Here, the sun vaults over the edge of the world,
Shining the windows, the loose silver and waiting shoes:
Do you shine the shoes: I will fill the empty pockets
And shine the good cloth: and the loose

Silver runs from us in streams.

The Force
and Other Poems

The Force

At Mrs Tyson's farmhouse, the electricity is pumped
Off her beck-borne wooden wheel outside.
Greased, steady, it spins within
A white torrent, that stretches up the rocks.
At night its force bounds down
And shakes the lighted rooms, shakes the light;
The mountain's force comes towering down to us.

High near its summit the brink is hitched
To an overflowing squally tarn.
It trembles with stored storms
That pulse across the rim to us, as light.

On a gusty day like this the force
Lashes its tail, the sky abounds
With wind-stuffed rinds of cloud that sprout
Clear force, throbbing in squalls off the sea
Where the sun stands poring down at itself
And makes the air grow tall in spurts
Whose crests turn over in the night-wind, foaming. We spin
Like a loose wheel, and throbbing shakes our light
Into winter, and torrents dangle. Sun
Pulls up the air in fountains, green shoots, forests

Flinching up at it in spray of branches,
Sends down clear water and the loosened torrent
Down into Mrs Tyson's farmhouse backyard,
That pumps white beams off its crest,
In a stiff breeze lashes its tail down the rocks.

Power

In a swirl of light he enters the house, in a thick collar
Braided to a cable broad as my body,
Is dangerous, and the snow tucked up around our windows.
Bubbles of light I dare say flick over him
If you touch one he crisps you
To batter. And this is the town's centre where he rides strongest
And thickest nearest his reactor
And the fringes are thinner and poorer.

Myself, for example, children skipping among my inside rooms,
Sit brooding across an outer room, feeling
Poor snow, poor birds, with the strong glass pellicle
Stretched over expanding weather. A swift mouser
Hurdles the frozen verges
With a torrent of gust
That turns the roofs
Like flicking a sheet
As if she alone kept the sun in reserve.
Power is everywhere, really.
We need only pluck up courage, and live
In a summery fashion – sun'd be out again.
It seemed to lighten as she ran,
It lives because we shine; at the flick of a switch

Power plunges through my house again.
The broad-blooded mammals on the backs of the moors,
They, too, contribute to it,
Huddled like bubbles slip in the torrents
Of crystallizing air,
Each with a spark of him
Igniting its bloods till death, and ovaries
Twinkling like a starry sky,
With heat at the centre and fright at the fringes.
See, this snow is tunnelled twistingly,
Leads to a lofty cool hutch
Overspangled with clustered eyes, heat at the centre
White fright at the fringes,
Twinkling like a starry sky as breath freezes.
We rose out of magma where power put his finger,
And the lines show,
Drifts of white flesh, thick roots of hot blood
Thrust in together.

Love-gate it is called, and love comes through it,
Though survival comes first.
Mere physique of love winds warm for days
And its cable limp at my knees – it's as if
The sun fed on me, and the food glad-hearted.

New Forms

I see all this new matter of the snow
Across this window, how it limps
Gently along and down, not like
A snow-storm or tempest, but like breeding.
And a light wind takes it gently with new shapes
And pats and moulds over the last new shapes
Of cricked branch and jagged verge,
Over tallow and bosses of the first ice
And greybeard stubble and thronging bracken of the first frost —
How it bats, bounces, tosses, scribbles, flings, cancels,
Writes out afresh round the wall of the house
In settled draughts unsettled forms
Leaping and twinkling over the gates,
Like our thoughts of the unborn
Crowding the old light
Belly fringed and curving like an horizon.

The Young Forester Protests

He's a pearly shell with a spirit nagging in it.
In our all packed sand-to-stone-upon-stone
He stares through stony glasses across a polished desk
Of cut wood. Killed wood lines the floors and walls,
I tread over trees' corpses, jointed. He lifts
A sliver of forest-flesh who cannot raise a tree
And writes with soft stone over bleached tree-skin

64

My arboreal answers.
                         Arboreal examinations.
I must pass with honours, or I can't stay.
I pass with honours. Young growth
Tipped at the bent dark conifers
Gives me right answers. This pebbled person
Needs its death so much he raises his forest

And honours me, a little. Meanwhile
Great trunks of leaves lift up thick and persistent,
Flinch in fining branches up
As though they loved but could not bear the sun.

I See

I see a man and that man is myself
Standing in the trees in a downpour cloudy with rush
Who penetrates the soft swarming element with his senses alive.

He is aware of the wet apples,
They snag like a rosy mist in their orchards;
He is aware of the spray of the rain running like sharp white mist
Across running white mist, which is the spray of the grasses seed-
    ing;
He watches the crows stepping within a white bubble of watershed,
    a dome,
How they fletch the sopping mud deeply as they step forward,
    which closes again;
(The look of them sounds of wet grain creaking deep in crammed
    bowels;)
He stoops easily and notices a bug embracing a grass-bole:

It peers through the green gloss at the heavy sap-veins stiff with
    their flow,
He sees its mouth-awls working with excitement for the plunge,
And he sees it fuss back again stout with its eggs; (a water-load
    shatters nearby and the green mother starts to stillness;)
Now I feel manly and that man is myself
Digesting his dinner in his study after dinner
Digesting my drinking and my senses are confirmable and shut
With purple wine-drapes more magnificent than the rags at my
    window,
And I have the small hard globe of dinner warm under my clasped
    hands
And I ask myself without impatience (for impatience is an out-
    door thing)
Who is that man who can stand in the rain and get his feet wet
And spit a cherrystone out into a weed-clump believing it will
    spring
Of his mouth, having warmed it and started the small germ mov-
    ing,
And who is that man I ask no who is that boy who is he
A good dinner hurt nobody and drink is nutritious and wears off,
And I resolve to begin my exercises again after breakfast
As those tight-bellied crows are all fluttering underground
And in my belly tug and flutter as though picked to and fro by the
    wheat-roots.

The House in the Acorn

Ah, I thought just as he opened the door
That we all turned, for an instant, and looked away,
Checked ourselves suddenly, then he spoke:
"You're very good to come," then,
Just for a moment his air thickened,
And he could not breathe, just for the moment.
"My son would have been glad that you came,"
He extended his thick hand, "Here, all together —"
We are not ourselves or at our ease,
I thought, as we raised our glasses, sipped;
"Help yourselves, please. Please . . ."

"If anyone would care . . ." He stood by the table
Rapping his heavy nails in its polished glare,
"My son is upstairs, at the back of the house,
The nursery, if anyone . . ." I studied
Stocky hair-avenues along my hand-backs,
Wandered through grained plots dappled and sunlit;
"My son . . . sometimes I think they glimpse
Perhaps for a while through sealed lids a few faces
Bending in friendship before it all fades . . ." I nodded,
Slipped out, face averted,

And entered oak aisles; oaken treads
Mounted me up along oaken shafts, lifting me past
Tall silent room upon tall silent room:
Grained centuries of sunlight toppled to twilight
By chopping and fitting: time turned to timber
And the last oak enclosure with claws of bent oak
Where his white wisp cradled, instantaneous,

Hardly held by his home in its polished housetops.
A breath would have blown him; I held my breath
As I dipped to kiss . . .

Now the instant of this house rolls in my palm
And the company spins in its polished globe
And the drawing-room reels and the house recedes
(Pattering dome-grained out of the oak)
While, ah, as I open the door I hear their close laughter,
Cool earrings swing to the gliding whisper,
More apple-cup chugs from the stouted ewer.

Misty Shore

Long shores soaking into the mist, birds
Howling into the mist, heaped
Creams of sensation hollowing in caress
Of winds tossing down, tearing
Corridors of mist; the white
Water-torrent towers into its echoes.

A puff of clarity passes . . . then mist
Reassembles the echoes, zones
Of smell rip over the skin, I see
Limp clouds and swag mouths sway deliberately.

Bowed

Rain from two directions, criss-cross,
Beat upon his head like a net, it beat
And he bowed his head and wept,
Caught by the head in this net.
He shook with the chill, I think.
He gasped with the shock.

The humour of a man out and caught
In wet weather, unbolting to the rain? Did it
Twinkle his ribs and spout from his beard?
Did he let heaven do his weeping for him
While he had a good chuckle under it, for once?

The Ferns

The ferns, they dip and spread their fronds
With moisture easy through the stems,
Green moisture, that interior wash
Of living sugars. Spores dehisce.

Under the baking sun, they breathe
In currents, swirls and soundless gasps
Though you below here, standing idle,
Perceive no influence. Sun rifts the clouds,
Ferns die and breathe, arch and curl,
Breathe and remake their forms above,
Are clouds, that spread and dip their fronds,

Unravel fingers and moisture-banks
Of filigree bracken. All's water.
All stoops and curls with water, gathers, droops

And doles the ferns their green moisture
Five miles down there on the baking earth,
And dunks the ferns in green moisture.
Spores dehisce. The ferns are breathing.
Then frost descends, like thronging ferns.

The Contentment of an Old White Man

The sky is dead. The sky is dead. The sky is dead.
I'm an old white man, if that is your opinion I'm content.
The fat white clouds roll in the old dead sky
They do me good, for all you say they're dead.
They pat my brow. They sweat me a little wet, perchance.
Just as my dazzling beard parades my cheeks, they give me
Ornament. I'm an old white man as well . . .
Dead indeed! You're a sack of wet yourself.
Step on them? Can *you* support the stroll of a razor?
They loll over my brow and childer my thoughts,
Or think I think them, so fond I am – not water-curds,
Thoughts! and correspondence! Dead skins and scurfs
And water-curds . . . but see how fatherly the sunset looks.
They rain, they pass into the ground, you piss,
You pass into the ground, I do, I know my kin,
My great kin, as a microbe is my lesser. Oh,

Lower a little shower and feel some roots, I say,
You've not slept in a bed at my age till you've wet it.
They pass and snort and snow, I'll catch my death
Squatting under a rainshower and pass away
At 105° all rubicund like a sunset. We're all kind,
All water, they're a little quicker, which means
Cleverer, sometimes, don't it? Oh and ah
The graceful fruity woods, cabby! of the clouds,
Snow running on snow and bending as it deepens.
I see I coach among them, my breath sends out;
These woods on mountains, we send up shapes together
Ridge upon ridge, offering them, these clouds,
The only things large enough for God to watch
And judge from, we'd better get there fast. I'm halfway
Being an old white man and here the tree-heads straighten
Slowly and slowly leaf again as
Flickers of white drop off them and
Slowly straighten heads hurting with spring
As their white dreams leave them. Cabby! the clouds rise
Because the sun wants them. Each cloud is unique.

The Affliction

Well, we face it out at last, do we,
Spots, and a very-ragged-countenance,
A race of spots cascading down our cheeks,
Floral cascades. One night long ago
I sank deep inside and looked out through my skin,
Through mild eruptions, lightly-tattered world.
I peered, out through the small fires,

Through shallow smouldering craters as they sank
And shifted in their sticky coals,
Flared orange, or expired in grit, and saw,
Throught the drifting smoke of half-damped bonfires saw,
Or thought I saw the . . . it was the . . . I knew I saw the . . .
My skin writes and rewrites what I thought I saw.

Dialogue in Heaven

A round, hollow, laughing silence,
A bony circlet.
Then the silence sneers,
The darkness becomes visible.
It's a man! We stoop, listening to his brains.

Fighting, fighting, he says,
Fighting all the time.
The cloud-canopy, soft textures
Gliding through great pores, the moon
Bounds into the sky!
I shall forget all this . . .
Fighting, fighting to remember.

Describe this darkness: a lanky
Tall man with his hair long
Who sweats exceedingly; an animal
Pacing the interface between us and the hot fires.

Why should he live at all?

Madam! the feelings!
Streaming brow and greasy nose are feelings.
Why, you, who are body of light
And whose movement is a thought,
You who can pass through this matter like mist,
Who draw with men's bodies, surely
Your pity rescues him!
Yes. Yes. It does.
I am tired with my love.
He knits his brow:
Mere strain over a surface;
It lights up his brains. Doll-lovers,
Tired, loving; the gods of men—
The idiots of heaven.
We love; what can we tell them?
They ask, "Are we immortal?"
We reply, "Unfortunately not." ... ?
And what of ourselves? Loving, tired.

The fields flame around; the scarecrow,
His smooth straw-head suddenly guffaws in a great ghast of light,
He shakes with hard laughter down into idiotic loose ashes.

Human Beam

Hot laughter-coughing drunkard,
The dark tree of the blood flexes
Slender and minutely-fashioned until death;
Rejoices, with the hammer-stroke at its roots,

Both pump and measure of time. Whatever
The man does in which it lives, it's buzzing
And fussing always at its tips with life delivered warm.
He is like the weather to it and the tree endures
The cloudy coughings and pourings of poison
And the voice and the laughter shaking and shaking its fruits
Swinging warm and ever-ripe at his knees,
To the height of its endurance:

The human forest is always ripe
And in a cloudy vapour of its humanity
Walks switching about the earth
With suspended in it nails and teeth
That gnash down to the trellis of bone;
Again and again they rise from their fruit,
Afraid for their fruit, proud of their rejoiceful pumping.

The Heir

Now here I am, drinking in the tall old house, alone,
The wide brown river squandering itself outside,
And there's a fine smell of cane chairs and conservatory dust here,
With the mature thick orchards thriving outside,
And I am drinking, which is a mixture of dreaming and feeding,
Watching how the stone walls admit all their square glad answers
To the sun that is alive and thriving outside,
And rests folded in a full pot of beer brimming before me now.
Or it could have been cider, agreed, because of our thriving
   orchards,

But it is beer, because of the brewery just down the way
Sipping at the wide brown river all the year round.
So I am a feeder and dreamer both
Of firm thriving apples and of the wide river outside
And of the sun that arrives and rests gladly, folded in my food.

And I agreed to that, and to the passing of the days,
With winged lips of the mist streaming at night, and in the morn-
    ing
Thick mists grinding themselves thin, and grinding themselves to
    nothing,
For mothers murther us by having us, naturally, and I am glad to
    be alive,
Drinking, with the beer squandering itself inside,
Sun folded in upon me and cider thriving among the trees,
And as I am a living man, Mother, I bear you no kind of a grudge,
Not to you, nor to the good kind cider or beer
Killing me and having me, for you agreed to die, and bear me no
    grudge
For being alive and dying, and dying much as you did . . .

So I'm glad to sit dreaming and feeding at the wide cane table set
For a solid meal that never comes, glad to be spending myself
As the river spends, and the sun pours out, and the ripe fruit
    splits,
Smiling juice sweetly to the hacking wasps, and you did as you
    agreed
Which was to give me life, and I agree to that too
For the beer agrees with me as I said, and I undertake
To go on agreeing so long as there's passage in my throat.

Sweat

I sit in the hot room and I sweat,
I see the cool pane bedew with me,
My skin breathes out and pearls the windowpane,
Likes it and clings to it. She comes in,
She loves me and she loves our children too,
And still the sweat is trickling down the pane,
The breath of life makes cooling streaks
And wobbles down the pane. We breathe and burn,
We burn, all together in a hot room,
Our sweat is smoking down the windowpane,
Marks time. I smoke, I stir, and there I write
PR, BR, a streaming heart.
The sun strikes at it down a wide hollow shaft;
Birds swing on the beams, boil off the grass.

Directive

Attend to the outer world.
See the calm delicate spray of the branches,
Watch the cool grey spurs of the sky
Sliding volumes the one over the other,
Listen, not inwardly to that gravel-crunch
(Yourself strolling over your nature,) but
Listen and wait, for,
Falling over the springy testing boughs,
The sliding volumes of the clouds and roads,
Out of the light clear rain shed,

Out of the open hot throat
The world attends you
Like a friendship, in three clear notes
Out of a bird's open throat.

Nothing but Poking

Those stamens bang like a pouch.
From what dimension of colour
Sea of formal patterning and sex
They poke their privy tongues about
In a public garden on Sunday.
They ought to be stopped, they're that rude.
Then I saw a spurt of seed
Dash past in yellow breeze, disgraceful,
Every one rubbing. They are everywhere
Like a pumping up of spirit, an omnipresence,
Flowers chill the sunlight.

Insulted, they put the sun away
By which they are seen.
It slides like a liner out to sea
Skimming the earth, a great wake of clouds.
We all tip backwards into gazing darkness.
Now the flowers will not be visible
Not until they've finished, then
The sun will rise in repleted colours.

Sunday Afternoons

I want a dew-keen scythe—
Peering or prodding into the puddles
Outlook reflections or shadows
I want a power-mower—
Banging about in all breezes
Shaggy thick heads without repose
Lolling about in the rain, doddering in it
I want shears—
Joyous colours for suffering in
And those wet red blooms like sliced tomatoes—
I want to get in there with a thick insulting stick.

If Only I Could
(In Autumn)

Sit watching the mouldy wood,
Bark peeling like old boots,
Blazed with white fleece,
Single-legged stools of pulp;
It becomes to him, he says, a luminous interior,
As though a dew-drop hoarded him,
Rinsed cleaner eyes and gave him
Light flowing at every damp point.
Each spike of a leaf of every leafy tree,
There, and elsewhere, scorched red by the season,
Measures at him and beams in his direction,
And where he is not he knows, he says,

Other dewed forests receive and shine light
In beds of light at every flashed tree-top,
In every forest needles lacing in every direction,
And the quiet blazes there as it does for him here, he says.

Noise

Suddenly in this dream I was printer's ink
Poured through the presses, patterned in every man's mind,
Ideas lodged in his farthest recesses were mine,
Had taken in my angular black, the engrams
Of my pain under the presses.

Now I revenge, for when one dies
I let him see it all clearly, all that he's learned
Now in its entirety for the first time known,
Laid in front of his soul's eye, painfully learned . . .

Then lightly, laughingly, carelessly I withdraw my spirit.
Letters, sentences, paragraphs shudder and mingle, a little black
    smear
Replaces each most delicate printed utterance,
A little ragged black snigger like a smudge

That bites like a scorched hole, spreading,
And each book blackens with thick noise
Full of the cries of the words lost in it.
And the libraries! They haemorrhage from their stacks.

79

So you would do well never again to read books
Nor to build up your children's brains on foundations of books
For it is a bookless pain and it lacks pictures
And it is an ocean of night-pain and noise.

Required of You this Night

A smoky sunset. I dab my eyes.
It stinks into the black wick of the wood.

Sparks wriggle, cut. I turn my back.
And night is at my frosty back.

I turn again. All stars!
It's bedtime.

There's no sky in my dreams, I dream none.
I work for sky, I work by sprinting up,
Breathing, sprinting up, and one star appears.

I chase it. It enlarges and I wake.
Dawn climbs into the sky like black smoke with white nails.

It's compact with the day's sharpness.
I'll dry my sopping pillow in it.
How long'll that take? I guess till sunset.

And then it sinks
All befrogged into that white glare.
The night is at my back instantly,
Draughty, and no star at all.
I weep again. I weep again frankly.
Sleep is nothing when you do it,
And nothing but a prim smile,

Except you're fighting to pull the sun down
That may not come unless you fight
Not for you anyway, Peter.

The Absolute Ghost

Well, in good time you came and gave it, God,
Rest of a kind in the mansions
That lapped at my feet like a watery hound,
And friendship feigned—that's dangerous!
At my feet the fissure yawned,
Long, low and cold the lake invited
Visitors to its mists, and I, in my draperies
Dressed like mist came, while the reeds
Parted like opening arms for me to go in.
Like opening arras. In dungarees next
They came to drag, the colour of mud;
In draperies I floated, the colour of ghosts
My substance licking every corner of where I was
To know it as I was known—then I was legion
There in the glades of the great lake
Whose lightest lilt of current, consent,
Moved us into a mansion. No breath
But the breathing of the current in which we were riven.
We passed, we passed, I did my job as matter
As I tried my mental, but not enough;
See, this slime-slide opening under her heel
Is where I ended, is me,
Spat out by some fish,
Among the crowds of small evils.

Really Gone

Well, you see, he got up off his couch in the open window and walked into the wood. The wood.

I know he was longing to ruck the appearance of things aside as he had rucked the curtain off the morning. Night had taken him no further; he dreamed no sky; he came to no conclusions. He had to pass through the appearance of things. Of the things.

He was to be justified, I think. His mother came in just before he went with a tray of poached eggs, toast, butter, salt. He ransacked the two eggs like shallow soft purses, the toast he left untouched, thin brittle sheets, two-dimensional, he had unscrewed the salt-cellar and poured the dry savoury powder over a clean plate: I imagine him peering into the side of every crystal as into a pane of window-glass; a crystallography text-book lay open on the carpet: pages were ripped from it and scattered as from a fit of anger. Anger. He ate nothing.

Action. His every action was governed by this search. Even women seemed too shallow; the one fine deep girl he knew had refused him because he could see no deeper. He knew his shallowness, and searched. Searched.

I hated the role of priest, but he fascinated me with his handicap. Would that I had been a doctor! Then I could have sent him back to childhood. To pick up threads. But I am plump and stable – this for him was *depth* – and I sufficed. I was cross very occasionally ... then he would say, with a full-fed look, that he had got beneath my skin. Skin.

The world seemed filmed, as with a skin. People drooped palely in his company, but this was the reflection of the discomfort they caused him. The cause. But, like the vampires of legend, he must have stepped up out of his time to become some animal like the fast and skittering bat or the fevered bird "whose grace is combustion"; or stepped down from human time to stand like a tree. For he had gone, there was no trace. He must have broken some skin, become a pebble, or faster-flowing like a stream. Or a lofty cyclone, slow-searching the waters. Or a mountain glittering with the thaw. Or a cherry-stone. Or a tree. Out of our time.

Our time. For, from wherever he is, he has begun to draw his things after him. First, our memories of him, leaving only the clearest things, an attitude, a habit of unpeeling and peering at the parcelled seeds of a flower, a gesture, but like a line-sketch on the glass, of pausing and clearing his throat by a mirror. And his poems begin to fade, which is why I write this memoir, which itself fades as I write. And this shows only that it is properly addressed to where he is living. Living.

The Widower

Yawning, yawning with grief all the time.
The live ones are often alive in fragments
And some of us scream as the weather changes.
Or I raise a frequent steak to my pluming nostrils,
Starving, or yawning, so hungry for air,
Gasping for life. And a snowflake was her friend.
And the sky of clouds hurrying and struggling
Beyond the skylight, were her friends.
She was daytime to the mind,
A light room of trees, spray of water, high flowers
Over a cloudscape, and I brought her
Twelve-hour lyings down for fear of this world,
Head buried in pillows for perfect darkness,
And into this she walked with nothing but advice
And what I called her spells for company.

Ah well, no doubt such happens to many.
Now I myself am alive only in fragments,
A piece of uncertain, of filthy tattered weather.
Pull the clothing to shreds; huddle the tatters together,
Wild and horrible! easily in my rags.

But you said, take another look!
Watch the mixtures, the things moving with one another,
Water running across running water, wind woven on it,
A sudden bleat of black birds marking across the marshes,
Beating wind across water, rooms built of glimmer and mist there.
I don't say it wouldn't have worked in time,
But my brow knitting it was lighted up my brain,
Mere strain over a surface,
And I just couldn't believe anything, anything at all.
Now look at me!

There's always something there, you said; now let me try
(That leaden waterspout searching so thick and tall
Over the mincing sunny water is no good to anyone)
Some vista of life, some mentality, so let me try now,
Something to watch always, and it's called your spell,
So what do I notice now in my nice quiet room
With the mullions and the college table and the books?
Why, look, there's that exciting queasiness
That queasy vividness of dark windows before thunder:
So I cross over quickly and there I am!
Up among them, the bad clouds over the bright blue,
Adjusting my black pieces over the innocent cricketers
Who tremble like white splinters in the deep gulfs beneath me,
Through the rifting thick platforms. . . . I quite enjoyed that—
But it wasn't true, was it?

All lies, and here the lies come again,
The dead, and the inventions of the dead,
The night, and what the night contains,
The great quivering jelly of resemblances,
The spreading, the too-great majority,
Whose heads hang from memories and nausea,
Who stroll about vomiting, shaking and gaping with it,
Who goggle in terror of their condition, who retire at dawn
To almost inaudible thin quarrels up and down the graveyard
    strata
Who lurk with invisible thin whines like gnats in daytime
But who billow through the deep lanes at dusk
Like a mist of bleached portraits, who do not exist,
Who walk like a shivering laundry of shifted humanity
And who stink. . . .

Not true! But thank God the day's come again,
A sunny warm day, a good morning, a morning to recline,
To wear shirts, to look simple and true,

To run hands with definite pleasure
Over the shorn bristly lawn full of mentality,
To plunge conjecture
Easily in a bold search for truth through the lawn's surface,
To consider the small kin, and their place in nature,
The spires and sinews of the worm, how excellent!
Dragging the long cold chain of life for itself,
And the cold speed of its terror,
And the drops of itself massaging into the corridor.
How it spreads under the harrow with no cry!
How it breaks into the bird's beak!
And what sublime sleep, oh marvellous fortitude,
Ever could breed these quiet pallid delving fancies?

And it was joy, one tells me, joy to die,
Moaning and tugging in terror of her condition,
With a thin grip around my ankle out of the turf,
Sinking into the majority, wobbling reminiscences,
And here they come again! because it's the nighttime,
Gelatinous bundles nozzled with portraits
Unconvincing and terrifying, but how many lie there!

You never actually saw one, do you think it's true?
Look for the truth in the lawn, one said, and I don't doubt she's
    found it.
Now somebody melts . . . but thinking of death got them this way
That's what you're saying, in these environs,
These parts of the mind, any mind, these fancies,
Thinking of horrors created them horrors.
Love frightens them, so let's frighten them.
It frightens them because it's so mysterious.
It frightens me. You are a shapely white.
Oh, I droop with admiration. No, no, I spring!
That kills them . . . and are you really there?
Yes, especially there. What happens then?

It makes them so thin. They are gone from themselves.
Did I frighten you then? Everyone fears.
Two is a round reality. Dead is a nonsense.
But a real one. And one of us is dead.

Decreator

Grown-up idiot, see the slow-motion of him,
And that slow-motion sludge of a tongue
Coiling along its stream of happenings,
Head lolling and tongue lolling,
Sudden brightenings, lurches. He was brisk,
Carried his headpiece like a haughty dish,
Suddenly his brain churned thick
And with a dull chime his brain turned over
A clucking and he sat down suddenly.
His poll curdled with a dull clack,
Cocked listening, a crooked cork of the neck,
A lid flipped. Not a spatter of larks
Rising, cheerily callous and irresponsible, nor melodramatic
Red entrails labouring, living brain split
All over, like a hairnet, bolting out of the ears—
Though the red mouth chewed, clack,
And the raw eyes soaked suddenly—
But a dull cluck and a dull kind of clay twisted
And skeined into a surprise and twirled up to
And round and round a wide stare.

Thereafter he was to wander
With a hesitation at either elbow
And a little free-wheeling spittle
Through a kind of pastoral, in the parks of patrons,
By their dusty greenhouses, bubbling glassy streams,
Springing up in odd corners, by snivelly taps,
Serious avenues. Their doves
Would babble off their lawns at him, their crones
Croon to him over the spinning,
Their tapping blind pensioners fall nodding as he came up to them

Leaky-lipped, faulty, and no part of it at all.
For one ordinary Sunday strolling
He looked down himself as with a dull crash
His brain fell several floors and stopped
And he sat down suddenly. It was a glance
From the sinewy confident husband and the rolling pram
Hooded like a whelk and pearly, started it, its scrap
Of white meat and fluff lodged in recesses and the woman
Fluffed on the man's arm
Like a floss of him, and he an elbow of her,
And the face-bone with its marrow of eyes,
Stare-marrow, and the lurking look in the whelk,
The same look, and all six with the one stare,
One flesh with six eyes, one person
In three stares, and the creation all rolled of it,
And he looked down himself and the creation trundled
Uphill at him and he looked
Down at himself and he sat down
Suddenly and his brain dropped several storeys
Burst the front door and pitched away downhill.

The Case

(for Roy Hart)

"Man . . . is an experiment and a transition. He is nothing else
than the narrow and perilous bridge between nature and spirit.
His innermost destiny drives him on to the spirit and to God. His
innermost longing draws him back to nature, the mother. Between
the two forces his life hangs tremulous and irresolute."

Hermann Hesse: *Steppenwolf*

I am a gardener,
A maker of trials, flowers, hypotheses.
I water the earth.
I raise perfumes there.
Mother told me to stand, and I did so,
Stepping towards the window in which she sat.
"Now, did you find him, your other half?
And mine," she said, and I shook my head:
"No, my time is so short and I'll take no oath."
"You've just taken one, by standing,
My dear one," she said, and she told me how the stars
Had said as much, and I concurred and saw
How the crystalware of the polished table,
The cabinets of glass things walling the room,
The tall roses beyond the glass, the gloss of the table,
Had said as much in sunshine from my first tottering.
So she lifted my hand and kissed it and said I was to be celibate,
And this was great good fortune and I was a good child
For I had a quest and few had as much.
The roses nodded.

So I became a gardener,
A maker of prayers, flowers, hypotheses.
A gardener "washed in my fertile sweat,"
My hair of an opulent brown "like the Lord's,
That makes you think of fertile fields."
And among the flowers, in the walled garden, "This is life!" she
    cried,
"What a shame, oh what a shame," she said,
"What a shame we have to die," she cried, all
The flowers pumping and pumping their natures into her,
Into her nostrils, winged wide, she leaning,
Leaning back, breathing deeply, blushing deeply,
Face shining and deep breath and tall brick
Holding the air still and the heat high in a tall room.

And I swam in the thunderstorm in the river of blood, oil and
cider,
And I saw the blue of my recovery open around me in the
water,
Blood, cider, rainbow, and the apples still warm after sunset
Dashed in the cold downpour, and so this mother-world
Opened around me and I lay in the perfumes after rain out of
the river
Tugging the wet grass, eyes squeezed, straining to the glory,
The burst of white glory like the whitest clouds rising to the sun

And it was like a door opening in the sky, it was like a door
opening in the water,
It was like the high mansion of the sky, and water poured from the
tall french windows.
It was like a sudden smell of fur among the flowers, it was like a
face at dusk
It was like a rough trouser on a smooth leg. Oh, shame,
It was the mother-world wet with perfume. It was something
about God.
And she stood there and I wanted to tell her something and she
was gone.
It was something about God. She stood smiling on the wet verge
And she waited for me to tell her but she was gone.
And three gusts of hot dry air came almost without sound
Through the bushes, and she went. Through the bushes
Of blown and bruised roses. And she went. And the bushes were
blown
And the gusts were hot, dry air, nearly black with perfume,
Alive with perfume. Oh shame. It was like an announcement,
Like an invitation, an introduction, an invitation, a quick smile in
the dusk.
It was like a door opening on a door of flowers that opened on
flowers that were opening.

It was like the twist of a rosy fish among lily-pads that were
    twisting on their deep stems.
The rosy goldfish were there in the dusky pond, but she was gone.
It was something about God. My hand made a wet door in the
    water
And I thought of something I knew about God. My mother
Stared at me from the pool over my shoulder and when I turned
    she was gone.
Then the wind blew three hot dry gusts to me through the broken
    rose-bushes
And she came to me dusky with perfume and I walked toward her
And through her, groping for her hand. And it was something
    about God.
And I searched in my head for it with my eyes closed. But it was
    gone.

And I became a gardener, a hypothesiser, one who would consult
    his sensations,
For "we live in sensations and where there are none there is no
    life,"
One with the birds that are blue-egged because they love the sky!
With the flocks of giraffes craning towards the heavens!
With the peacocks dressed in their love for the high sun
And in their spectra of the drifting rains, one
With the great oaks in my keeping that stretched up to touch God!
And one who could look up gladly and meet God's gaze,
His wide blue gaze, through my blood, as I think;
And God was silent and invisible and I loved him for it,
I loved him for his silent invisibility, for his virile restraint,
And I was one with my peacocks that sent out their wild cry
Sounding like shrill "help!" and meaning no such thing,
While my flocks of deer wrote love in their free legs
Their high springy haunches and bounding turf. And they would
    pause
And look upwards, and breathe through wide nostrils, and all day

It was wide and firm and in God's gaze and open: tussock and
    turf, long lake,
Reed-sigh, silence and space, pathway and flower furnace
Banked up and breathing.

And the people. And the causeway into the walled garden.
And the people walking in so slowly, on their toes
Through the wide doorway, into the cube of still air,
Into the perspective of flowers, following each other in groups,
Gazing around, "Oh, what shame, to die!" and the great doorway
And ourselves, smiling, and standing back, and they changed,
Concentrated, concentrating, at the edges of the body, the rims
Tighter, clearer, by the sensations of their bodies, solidified, bound,
Like the angels, the bodies' knowledge of the flowers inbound
Into its tightening and warming at the heart of flowers, the fire
    called
"Then-shall-ye-see-and-your-heart-shall-rejoice-
And-your-bones-shall-sprout-as-the-blade. . . ."

And she was gone. And she lay down like the earth after rain.
It was love-talk in every grain. And something about God.
The brick walls creaked in the wind, grain to grain.
And judgment came as the father comes, and she is gone.
Clouds swoop under the turf into the pond, the peacock cries
"Help!" strutting in its aurora, love talks
Grain to grain, gossiping about judgment, his coming. Ranges
Tumble to boulders that rattle to shingles that ease to wide beaches
That flurry to dust that puffs to new dusts that dust
To dusting dust, all talking, all
Gossiping of glory, and there are people
In the gardens, in white shirts, drifting,
Gossiping of shame through the gardens, "Oh glory!"

Through the gardens. . . . Well, father, is that how you come?
Come then.

Whose breath is it that flares through the shrubberies?
Whose breath that returns? Look at the people
All ageing to judgment, all
Agreeing to judgment. Look at that woman
Still snuffing up the flowers. My mother!
Look at her. She bends backwards to the tall flowers, falls.
Her flower-laden breath returns to the skies.
I think this garden is a prayer,
Shall I burn it as an offering?
And I think these people are a prayer,
I think they are a message.
Shall I burn them for their syllable?
There is a fire crying "shame!" here already!
It mixes dying with flowering.
I think we husk our uttering. I think
We tip it out. Our perfect syllable,
Tripped out over the death-bed, a one,
Round, perfectly-falling silence.
Look how they seek the glory over these flowers!
I wanted to say something about God,
My syllable about God. I think
We are a prayer. I think
He wants his breath back, unhusked
Of all the people, our dying silences.
Our great involuntary promise
Unhusked, flying out into the rain, over the battlefields,
Switching through shrubberies, into the sky. . . .

You press, oh God!
You press on me as I press on an eyeball,
You press sunsets and autumns and dying flowers,
You press lank ageing people in gardens "Oh shame
To die," you feather roses and matchflames like wisps of your
    fingers,
Your great sun cuffs age at us. I will bring,

I will bring you in, father, through the bounds of my senses,
Face to face, father, through the sockets of my head,
Haul you in, father, through my eyes with my fingers,
Into my head through my eyes, father, my eyes, oh my eyes. . . .

To live in the blind sockets, the glorious blunt passages,
Tended by gardeners, nostril, eye, mouth,
Bruised face in a white shirt ageing,
To be called "Father" and to hear call high
"Oh shame, what a shame, to die" as they see the great flowers,
To hear the peacock "help!" that means no such thing,
And to live unseeing, not watching, without judging, called
    "Father".

Earth

By the hearth,
The discomfort of earth, time's fire,
Withers her. She shrinks
Into her eyes, which well and gleam,
Glitter with sleep, sink shut,
Fed by the dry runnels of her face.
The old apple shrivels, but,
For a while, the smell is sweet as blossom,
And the skin soft as warm flowers,
For, as I disturb her sleep, and rise to go,
This goodness wells from the warm eyes
Along the runnels, creating the face:

And as her eyes open and the world returns
So the wrinkles flood over her face
Like earth irrigated with kindliness.

Constant Praise

Frost and clarity at night.
Stiff, slick roadway. Its gorge's
Stars answer the night's gorges.
I skim across it rapidly in boots,
Give thanks, deliberately, in fright.

For walking is so easy, to drop, a thought.
Mist is blowing down the road in hoops,
And heaps and smokes until the road is bled.
I skim through clouds, not plunge, by grace,
Give thanks, deliberately, in fright.

A Picture

How delightful! A family picture.
Strong sons rub shoulders with fathers, thin grandfathers.
Daughters with round arms about mothers, blind grandparents.
A strong, many-storeyed building, firm-founded!

Here! the view dissolves. To what?
An advertisement, no less. A clothier's window
Where tall anonymous dummies, sober-suited,
Grasp their corresponding thick bolts of decent cloth.

Design

The designer sits, head in hand.
What costume could be better for battle, the more sensible?
Why, one blood won't mar.
I'll score it with scarlet.

But often men outlast deep wounds.
Some blood is old, and black.
Let's have a tatter, then, I slash scarlet black.

And here is a master-stroke. Let it be random tatter.
Random tables fed into the looms.
Thus as they advance none perhaps are wounded,

Or all are, mortally, and ripped from the field.
Horrible half-dry men.
Yes. Let them advance as though ripped from the clay.
One of the many patterns of battle.
And pipeclay features with blacking sockets, General.

97

On the Screaming of the Gulls

The wet wings of birds into the air
Making off from our roofs in the rain
Clapped hard to the drenched flank
In a spray of feather-wet
Must sting the sleek body as they clap.
The muscle-yoke across the back
Stings and spurs the armless animals
And spurs them until they scream
As they do, as they do all night
Whizzing into the mist like chain-shot
That howls where it strikes.
They are ridden upon by their wings,
By their ability for flight,
The wings enjoy the use of them,
Clapped tight around the panting heart.
Brute muscle is the brain, and the brain
In the slippery bright eyes
Mere watcher and recorder
Of muscles on the go, always,
Forcing screams from stung panting sides,
For fish, more fish, fish
Sustaining their spurts across the estuary,
For use, to enjoy the flight
Tight along their screaming mounts.
The gull is delighted in by others,
Ridden by other passengers, parcel of jockey-owners;
The sex jaunts from ground to breeding-ground,
The oval, perfect sex, the thinking egg
Skilled to spin them, bank, and keep their trim
In tight mating flocks
As though furnace were gyroscope,
Compass and owners' orders in one packet;

Compassionate more than the wings,
Mapping no ground, it gives, though the way is lost
Good company in payment.
The weary bird launches its neck
Over the grey rollers.

Cherry-seed, nematode, spore
Of bacilli without number, fern-, alga-spore
Ride too, rafted
To claw, feather, beak
Of this airship
Whose furnace-draught is screams,
Or grow folded into the grey bowel, bilge
And breeder too of the gull's own rotting
Just as it falls, log
Scattered, fluttered
Into unbound leafy bones
Or feathery bones suspended in rut,
Worked to the last instant, thin plans
Surviving pursy passengers.

The Sermon

Minister : Dearly beloved. I should say, Friends!

Coming events! God will roast the globe like a goose on a spinning spit, the tiny mites of men will lie enfolded and faceless in the crackling of its crust, he will come with his hot knives and trumpets and carve the steaming tender flesh of its rocks and lick them up with smacking lips of fire, the savoury crisp much praised in his mouth, and his coming, so great he is, will seem like the dripping upon us of galaxies before the fire takes us all. Repent! Repent!

Congregation : But you told us before that God suffered for us, that his face was webbed with tears for our loss.

Minister : I was coming to that.

Ah, brethren. In the fear and terror I struck you all with just then, in the gracious sweat I drew from under your hairlines like cool and pure spring water that leaps from a tap in clean arched crystal staves, in the shivers I clothed you with like sackcloth, it was but the fear of death I gave you to give you back again the appetite for life.

Appetite for life, friends . . . in all your pantings, your teemings, your pantings, the green roofs of your fields, the juices of the laid grasses, the soft beds of feathery hay in the sun and of haymaking feathers in the night-time, in all of these you may sometimes meet God—in the city's symphony of bedsprings on spring nights under the peppery sky twirling with stars, in the white soft babies waited on hand and foot, in the bedrooms and in the bedsprings . . .

Congregation : We don't understand at all. Didn't he make us? Isn't he above and beyond us? Doesn't he live in heaven, out there? If he's infinite how does he get into our houses? How does he know what goes on down here?

Minister : I was coming to that. Yes indeed, he is above and beyond us all. But how does he get to us, how does he know what goes on? Why, he feels the hydrogen bomb like a little prick in his foot; he knows it all through that little shard of awareness, of god-power, of *soul,* he put in each one of us—rather like the barb and bud of a nerve-ending to him. It is a bright crystal and splinter of understanding in each of us that he could not and would not destroy any more than he would pluck out one of his own all-working fingers.

Congregation: But then tell us why he came to earth, if he's within us each from birth.

Minister: I was coming to that.

If you poked your finger in an ants'-nest could *you* get a good idea of their lives, how they live? Would you suddenly become a sav-ant? No, you'd get bitten, and the teeming sooty little creatures would scuttle all up your wrist and down your shirt-collar and you'd have a hell of a picnic. In us, God is blistered and bitten by the ants'-nest of nature, its hissing acid teeth and lies, its dirt and greenery, its love and venery, its steaming hay-quilts and its uncovered and dangerous well-shafts. Every suicide is a nasty shock to him, every motor-smash a new toothmark, every rocket into the sky a little dart in his side.

We then are God's littlest fingertip, our world is formed and built up around him, our ploughed fields are his looped thumb-prints, so are our ridged and whorled streets, our roundabouts, our sweating neon circuses.

But—he visited all this, he visited it with his eyes, and left the heavens empty as concentration upon the pages of a book dims the stars. He held up, you see, the tips of his working fingers, they were smarting, they stung, he came to heal them, not to finger in the dark any more, but to see what he was doing for a moment—and may he not have been a little surprised by what he found on his fingers? It was as though he were riding a bicycle—look! no hands—and in his visitation had suddenly gripped the handlebars. And it's a *good* ride—look at our tools, our machines, our sky-scrapers, our friends of the American continent, our technical economy . . .

Congregation: How lovely! Now tell us again about the day of judgment. You tell it all so gloriously.

Minister: I was coming to that. And I will tell you what I see in my dreams.

It is the valley of dry bones. A dry, long valley. Heaped bones, like an ancient massacre. A dust-coloured sky, burning hot, coppery. Then, at the tip of the valley, a shaft of real sunlight, sunshine. It begins to cross the splintery ground towards me. A small white figure seems to carry it; it swings with him, like a caber. It is a naked child, a toddler, struggling over the burning rock. He picks his way over the scattered bones, and, in his wake, they stir, twitch, flip on their ends, and fly together like filings in a magnet's field, bone to bone. Sinews spread over them, flesh creeps upwards, eyelids blink on the flayed faces, and skin whitens and flexes there like hot milk. A host of them stands, and where they stand the young grass begins pricking through the rocky soil, so that soon they throng, and breathe, in a great green moist meadow, a mighty host of men and animals. Ezekiel 37.

Then the fleecy clouds in the new, blue, summery sky gather, and pile up and up into a great white chasm, and the naked child behind whom these hosts have sprung to life begins to climb up and up the bolstered clouds. Angels appear, with their staring golden eyes, nodding like sunflowers large as planets. The child totters up to eternity, past the steeps of the sky, past the hills of angels, and his eyes blaze with authority. Up and over (say) poor Mr Jackson, on his newly-assembled knees and wearing them out already. The infant is a boy, and strides higher, over the toad that has popped its thin white wits into their sockets to hear the angels sing, and has jumped back into its sloppy-throated skin. The boy is a youth who strides higher and higher, over our drowned dapper friend Pincher Martin, his bones rolled here by the sea, who shoves on the red-lined gloves of his hands, adjusts his heavy casque of bones and brains, and strolls out to kneel to the tiers of madrigalists, the Shining Ones piled over the sky with throats of power, that sing dead pigeons spurting out of the turf . . . and above all their heads the youth becomes a man, beard flickering at the lips, and the man strides up and beyond the limits of sight, up the white-hot rock-hard funnel of witnesses, to fetch his father . . .

Something is coming with a deep note . . .

Closing all eyes as it comes . . . both men and angels burst with praise as the father nears, nothing but sealed eyes and adoration in the fire of him, with the eschewment of flesh, and the basting of tears . . .

Congregation : This is good comfort. We tremble and glow. But what of comfort down here—below ?

Minister : I was coming to that precisely, to give you real and immediate comfort. Of such is the kingdom of heaven. Mark 10. And here is his special dispensation and mercy, the Secret, the innermost heart of the forest.

You think you're going to age, fall apart, get dusty and grey, smell, plunge into a wallow of decrepitude, a slough of incontinence, annoy little girls with rattling sweetiebags, wet your pants at the flash of a white skirt and the rumble of a baby-carriage with longing for the starchy lap of a young plump nursemaid, lose your tongue in your teeth mumbling old sockets for gamey meat-shreds and sit speechless, death's worst, winding-sheets, and tumbling to decay—but it's not so.

You see, *we live backwards* !

Haven't you noticed ? We start as angels, spirits, pure souls—little children. When we grow up—maybe not so good. And in some of us the orient and immortal wheat gets ground exceeding small. But we've got the memory of it. So isn't it best and wisest to have the reward first, so nothing can spoil it ? To live first and pay later ? I know you all must have many things at home you've bought without paying for. That television set ? The mortgage ? The very clothes you stand up in ? Feel the nap of the cloth. It's somebody else's. You're paying for it now. But nobody can take your childhood away from you. Your reward is safe. You've had it ! For I dare hazard a guess that there is nobody here who has not at some time, it may be in the distant past, it may be yesterday or last week, nobody who has not been a child of some sort or another. You may not quite make it when you're grown up, but never mind. Little angels.

Congregation: All this is a great comfort. But tell us, reconcile us to that bomb. It hovers over our heads like a spiteful thumb.

Minister: I was coming to that.

O, my dear, dear brethren and friends, let me once again appeal to you, let me try. Do not worry what happens to your flesh, your mere bodies. Go back to your lives, deliver your babies into their reward, it is God's work. Shift the lead out of your pants. What happens to your flesh, your tissues, can only a little rust the bright white metal of your souls, a little dust it, obfuscate, occlude, corrode, but only a little, constipate, tie it in knots, it cannot *kill* it, not even in the great blaze of pain, the sheet of lightning, the great sheet of agony, and remember it is God's pain, our blazing agony multiplied by our millions, for him. You have seen the dry burnt corpses of that agony with their poor cindered fists caught up like a boxer's. But God cannot die, and by the same token no more can we! Remember that whatever happens cannot hurt us, because we *are* God—not hurt us permanently, anyway. Brothers—and I am speaking to God—do not sit about wailing here for God's second-coming-before-it-is-too-late—he is already here, and We will be There, each of us a shard of him, a ward of him, a bright, piercing, secure, razor-sharp splinter of him, and heaven . . . where no moth nor rust . . . Matthew 6 . . . We are already Here . . . and More of Me arrives every day!

Congregation: We've had enough. This is blasphemy. You are Antichrist. You are the Devil. God is not mocked! In his own house too! And I saw a beast rise up out of the sea, having seven heads and ten horns, and upon his heads the name of blasphemy; and there was given unto him a mouth speaking great things and blasphemies. Revelation 13. You can't carry on like this in our church! You can't carry on like this in our church!

Minister: But I was coming to that—

What I am asking you to do, friends, IS to carry on before it is too late, before we are all snatched back to God from whom we came, and who frightens us so; before we're all snapped back like elastic, blown up back to God whom we will not understand, any more than the clippings understand the toenail; snatched back away from life as we know it—I am asking you, all of you, whoever you are, cutthroats, croupiers, cripples, blacksmiths, wordsmiths, birdsmiths, birdbathmakers, billiard-markers, in-patients, waiters, head-waiters, hairdressers, hairy or hairless, bright or stupid, good-headed or beheaded, I am asking you, friends, whatever it all means, whoever is right, whatever explanation we use—to—carry on, so *some* good can come of it, to carry on, to experiment, as I am doing, good my dear sweet world, to carry on, to carry on. . . .

Dr Faust's Sea-Spiral Spirit and Other Poems

Christiana

That day in the Interpreter's house, in one of his Significant
   Rooms,
There was naught but an ugly spider hanging by her hands on
   the wall,
And it was a spacious room, the best in all the house.
"Is there but one spider in all this spacious room?"
And then the water stood in my eyes
And I thought how like an ugly creature I looked
In what fine room soever I was,
And my heart crept like a spider.

And my heart crept like a spider into the centre of my web
And I sat bell-tongued there and my sound
Was the silvery look of my rounds and radii,
And I bent and sucked some blood, but I did it
With care and elegance like a crane unloading vessels;
I set myself on damask linen and I was lost to sight there,
And I hugged my legs astride it, wrapping the pearl-bunch
   round;
I skated on the water with legs of glass, and with candystriped
   legs
Ran through the dew like green racks of glass cannonball;
And I saw myself hanging with trustful hands

In any room in every house, hanging on by faith
Like wolfhounds that were dwarfs, or stout shaggy oats,
And I wept to have found so much of myself ugly
In the trustful beasts that are jewel-eyed and full of clean
    machinery,
And thought that many a spacious heart was ugly
And empty without its tip-toe surprise of spiders
Running like cracks in the universe of a smooth white ceiling,
And how a seamless heart is like a stone.
And the Interpreter saw
The stillness of the water standing in her eyes,
And said,
Now you must work on Beelzebub's black flies for Me.

For Barbara

Minerals of Cornwall, Stones of Cornwall

A case of samples

Splinters of information, stones of information,
Drab stones in a drab box, specimens of a distant place,
Granite, galena, talc, lava, kaolin, quartz,
Landscape in a box, under the dull sky of Leeds—
One morning was awake, in Cornwall, by the estuary,
In the tangy pearl-light, tangy tin-light,
And the stones were awake, these ounce-chips,
Had begun to think, in the place they came out of.

Tissues of the earth, in their proper place,
Quartz tinged with the rose, the deep quick,
Scrap of tissue of the slow heart of the earth,
Throbbing the light I look at it with,
Pumps slowly, most slowly, the deep organ of the earth;
And galena too, snow-silvery, its chipped sample
Shines like sun on peaks, it plays and thinks with the mineral
    light,
It sends back its good conclusions, it is exposed,
It sends back the light silked and silvered,
And talc, and kaolin, why they are purged, laundered,
As I see the white sand of some seamless beaches here
Is laundered and purged like the whole world's mud
Quite cleansed to its very crystal; talc a white matt,
Kaolin, the white wife of Cornwall
Glistening with inclusions, clearly its conclusions
Considered and laid down, the stone-look
Of its thoughts and opinions of flowers
And turf riding and seeding above it in the wind,
Thoughts gathered for millennia as they blossomed in millions
Above its then kaolin-station within the moor,
The place of foaming white streams and smoking blanched
    mountains.
Asbestos had found this bright morning
Its linear plan of fibres, its simple style,
Lay there, declaring, like the others;
Granite, the great rock, the rock of rocks,
At home now, flecked green, heavily contented in its box,
Riding with me high above its general body,
The great massif, while its fellows, the hills of it
Rise high around us; nor was lava silent
Now it remembered by glistening in this light
Boiling, and was swart with great content

Having seen God walking over the burning marl, having seen

A Someone thrusting his finger into the mountainside
To make it boil—here is the issue of this divine intrusion,
I am the issue of this divine intrusion,
My heart beats deep and fast, my teeth
Glisten over the swiftness of my breath,
My thoughts hurry like lightning, my voice
Is a squeak buried among the rending of mountains,
I am a mist passing through the crevices of these great seniors
Enclosed by me in a box, now free of the light, conversing
Of all the issue this homecoming has awakened in the stone
    mind
The mines like frozen bolts of black lightning deep in the land
Saying, and the edge of their imaginings cuts across my mind:
We are where we were taken from, and so we show ourselves
Ringing with changes and calls of fellowship
That call to us ton to ounce across Cornish valleys.

The valleys throng with the ghosts of stone so I may scarcely
    pass,
Their loving might crush, they cry our at their clumsiness,
Move away, death-dealing hardnesses, in love.
The house is full of a sound of running water,
The night is a black honey, crystals wink at the brim,
A wind blows through the clock, the black mud outside
Lies curled up in haunches like a sleeping cat.

The Moon Disposes
Perranporth beach

The mountainous sand-dunes with their gulls
Are all the same wind's moveables,

The wind's legs climb, recline
Sit up gigantic, we wade
Such slithering pockets our legs are half the size,
There is an entrance pinched, a plain laid out,
An overshadowing of pleated forts.
We cannot see the sea, the sea-wind stings with sand,
We cannot see the moon that swims the wind,
The setting wave that started on the wind, pulls back.

Another slithering rim, we tumble whirling
A flying step to bed, better than harmless,
Here is someone's hoofprint on her hills
A broken ring with sheltering sides
She printed in the sand. A broken ring. We peer from play.

Hours late we walk among the strewn dead
Of this tide's sacrifice. There are strangled mussels:
The moon pulls back the lid, the wind unhinges them,
They choke on fans, they are bunched blue, black band.
The dead are beautiful, and give us life.
The setting wave recoils
In flocculence of blood-in-crystal,
It is medusa parched to hoofprints, broken bands,
Which are beautiful, and give us life.
The moon has stranded and the moon's air strangled
And the beauty of her dead dunes sent us up there
Which gave us life. Out at sea
Waves flee up the face of a far sea-rock, it is a pure white door
Flashing in the cliff-face opposite,
Great door, opening, closing, rumbling open, moonlike
Flying open on its close.

Young Women with the Hair of Witches and no Modesty

"I loved Ophelia!"

I have always loved water, and praised it.
I have often wished water would hold still.
Changes and glints bemuse a man terribly:
There is champagne and glimmer of mists;
Torrents, the distaffs of themselves, exalted, confused;
And snow splintering silently, skilfully, indifferently.
I have often wished water would hold still.
Now it does so, or ripples so, skilfully
In cross and doublecross, surcross and countercross.
A person lives in the darkness of it, watching gravely;

I used to see her straight and cool, considering the pond,
And as I approached she would turn gracefully
In her hair, its waves betraying her origin.
I told her that her thoughts issued in hair like consideration of
    water,
And if she laughed, that they would rain like spasms of
    weeping,
Or if she wept, then solemnly they held still,
And in the rain, the perfumes of it, and the blowing of it,
Confused, like hosts of people all shouting.
In such a world the bride walks through dressed as a waterfall,
And ripe grapes fall and splash smooth snow with jagged
    purple,
Young girls grow brown as acorns in their rainy climb towards
    oakhood,
And brown moths settle low down among ivories wet with
    love.
But she loosened her hair in a sudden tangle of contradictions,

In cross and doublecross, surcross and countercross,
And I was a shadow in the twilight of her late displeasure
I asked water to stand still, now nothing else holds.

The Passengers

He and she, on separate trains, speeding to meet

Among them all, those heads
In windowed rows like rows of bibles, testimony bound
In skin and black hair, they seem the ones
Whose faces change, and their cigarette-smoke
Changes the same, as when a door to thoughts
Is shut or opened. Each one seems to think:

He: Why does the year turn round, and hand me ever
The same person? Now I can see
Every page in the book at once, she takes the book
And blows the print off, like a coarse black soot,
And the solid paper, thousand-walled white room,
Opens in banks of doors as she approaches.

She: Like our diaries lying wide open on empty pages
White with so many secrets we can't tell.

He: She turned to the window
Scarcely stirring in that dense silk dress
Filling her eyes with the moon deliberately
Brimming salt brooks buttoning the bright moon,
All dress and whiteness, nothing but the two,
Brilliant gaiety or white anguish.

She:　A moth, enthroned, with gold eyes
　　　And golden undershirt peeping from grey cloak
　　　Had settled on the window where I turned
　　　Blank from night with the moon full in my eyes to look
　　　　at him.

He:　The clock moans, strikes, and strikes again,
　　　The diaries lie wide open, filling me
　　　With so many secrets I can't tell, the unread books
　　　Lie like cold plates in greasy piles around me
　　　For the banks of print
　　　Were blown away at night-time, all we knew
　　　Clumped far off into a crow of such tragic blackness
　　　That when it settled on the branching stars
　　　I wondered they didn't snap and fall.

She:　I recall the deep hum of bees
　　　Raising their eloquent temple, how the wind moved
　　　With wings of black wheat, and all the stars beat
　　　Like pulses of the one body, as we lay
　　　Among the deep wheat, but I cannot remember
　　　It seems so long ago
　　　That start of beauty which in a moment
　　　Seemed to destroy all ordinary speech.

He:　Who was it that when I thought him coming
　　　I could stop it, and make the night
　　　Full of a smell of rotting stars, and my face
　　　A dead man's, where decomposition
　　　Starts with a look of sorrow?

She:　We are passengers, swift-stitched across the country,
　　　And as my train rushes into the tunnel
　　　Winged seeds fly backwards. Who
　　　Are we travelling to make, if anyone?

He: Nothing but gaiety or white anguish. We had seemed
      parents
      Presiding over the work's birth, now once again we're
      lovers
      Hurrying to a meeting, hasty lovers, or dead ones,
      or
      Convalescent lovers—we! convalescents!
      As I drove out
      Into the raiding thunderstorm
      A great thing, like a lion's head,
      Lifted into the sky, and I was myself
      Merely a little slime containing angels.

She: Blood has flowed, the danger's past,
      A tree is complicated when it's down,
      But now he rides into refreshed danger.

He: With visible emotion once more in the trees
      I shall lie down again
      And travel once again so far my memory
      Will fail in love-spreadings.

She: Will it rise this time on moss
      Heavy and green as soaked velvet sleeves, and flutter
      Like summer butterflies, or pump
      Like a great fat locust, and lose balance
      Like a fountain on itself for forgotten instants,
      None that we can tell? There are no sides
      And all is ritual, lover, we both ride
      These dancing cataracts of white. If the black blood
      Falls, the womb's blank and
      Danger's past and as the year turns
      It hands us ever the same person riding
      Into refreshed danger, not mine, not mine.

Both: Past these hundred bridges in their shaking stones
We rush against this blank wall
Like the great steam pile-cloud fretted with our speed
Hollowing away behind us, clearing. We follow
To dash against it, fountain
For a forgotten instant turned on and off and balanced
But springing in each season, followed.

The Youthful Scientist Remembers

After a day's clay my shoes drag like a snail's skirt
And hurt as much on gravel. You have mud on your jersey,
This pleases me, I cannot say why. Summer-yolk
Hangs heavy in the sky, ready to rupture in slow swirls,
Immense custard: like the curious wobbly heart
Struggling inside my pink shirt. Spring is pink,
 predominately,
And frothy, thriving, the glorious forgotten sound of healing,
And cheering, all shouting and cheering. With what inwardness
The shadows of autumn open, brown and mobile as cognac,
And the whole of my beer comes reeling up to me in one great
 amber rafter
Like a beam of the purest sun, well-aged; as it travels the grass
The dead smile an immense toothy underground, kindly.
I cannot explain why. You pointed out that the lily
Was somebody's red tail inside their white nightie
                              So much so
That I am still sober and amazed at the starlight glittering in
 the mud,
I am amazed at the stars, and the greatest wonder of them all

Is that their black is as full as their white, the black
Impends with the white, packing between the white,
And under the hives of silence there are swarms of light,
And padded between black comb, struggling white.

I cannot explain this, with the black as full as the bright,
The mud as full as the sunlight. I had envisaged
Some library of chemistry and music
With lean lithe scores padding the long pine shelves,
Plumage of crystal vials clothing strong deal tables;
Had thought that the stars would only tug at me slightly,
Or sprinkle thin clear visions about me for study—
Instead you point at that flower, your dress fits like a clove.

The Idea of Entropy at Maenporth Beach

"C'est elle! Noire et pourtant lumineuse."

A boggy wood as full of springs as trees.
Slowly she slipped into the muck.
It was a white dress, she said, and that was not right.
Leathery polished mud, that stank as it split.
It is a smooth white body, she said, and that is not right,
Not quite right; I'll have a smoother,
Slicker body, and my golden hair
Will sprinkle rich goodness everywhere.
So slowly she backed into the mud.

116

If it were a white dress, she said, with some little black,
Dressed with a little flaw, a smut, some swart
Twinge of ancestry, or if it were all black
Since I am white, but—it's my mistake.
So slowly she slunk, all pleated, into the muck.

The mud spatters with rich seed and ranging pollens.
Black darts up the pleats, black pleats
Lance along the white ones, and she stops
Swaying, cut in half. Is it right, she sobs
As the fat, juicy, incredibly tart muck rises
Round her throat and dims the diamond there?
It is right, so she stretches her white neck back
And takes a deep breath once and a one step back.
Some golden strands afloat pull after her.

The mud recoils, lies heavy, queasy, swart.
But then this soft blubber stirs, and quickly she comes up
Dressed like a mound of lickerish earth,
Swiftly ascending in a streaming pat
That grows tall, smooths brimming hips, and steps out
On flowing pillars, darkly draped.
And then the blackness breaks open with blue eyes
Of this black Venus rising helmeted in night
Who as she glides grins brilliantly, and drops
Swatches superb as molasses on her path.

Who is that negress running on the beach
Laughing excitedly with teeth as white
As the white waves kneeling, dazzled, to the sands?
Clapping excitedly the black rooks rise,
Running delightedly in slapping rags
She sprinkles substance, and the small life flies!

She laughs aloud, and bares her teeth again, and cries:
Now that I am all black, and running in my richness
And knowing it a little, I have learnt
It is quite wrong to be all white always;
And knowing it a little, I shall take great care
To keep a little black about me somewhere.
A snotty nostril, a mourning nail will do.
Mud is a good dress, but not the best.
Ah, watch, she runs into the sea. She walks
In streaky white on dazzling sands that stretch
Like the whole world's pursy mud quite purged.
The black rooks coo like doves, new suns beam
From every droplet of the shattering waves,
From every crystal of the shattered rock.
Drenched in the mud, pure white rejoiced,
From this collision were new colours born,
And in their slithering passage to the sea
The shrugged-up riches of deep darkness sang.

To John Layard

The Wizard's New Meeting

I am startled by comparisons.
Ice melts from the thatches with the bare restraint
With which the flesh disquantities.
The sound of it beats back like small hearts in sheer spaces.
Stars lie in pools black as pupils
That return their stare, ice-irised. Though nearby
Fire thaws out the greenwood, slow explosion
Of smoke lifts through the chimney, here

My slow trudge snaps snow-crust and prints white darkly;
Blanched breath trudges across the night sky.
Things shiver and my breath is negatived;
In spread hand I hold the pane.

I slam the door. The brazier sucks
And glows in storeys.
I have the hair, the wax, a specimen of writing,
A pane of ice from the flooded churchyard.
I cast them in, they begin to wreck
And flicker with thin films, a gold stain spreads.
What do I think will happen, but steam and smoke?
I utter the words of vertigo, were I so strong
I should vomit as I spoke them, as some are said to,
Vomit as a thorough utterance. I am unsuitable,
But I will lend it blood.

The great book opens of its own accord,
Its snow-light floods the room, it comes, it comes,
The past has ripped away, there is a thin snow curling
And recurling over jagged mines
Of reserved lightning, I see boiling eyes
And a puckered mouth shouting silence so I razor,
The bowl fills and I grow colder
And the squalling bends to sip. I will not speak in terror
For looks of terror terrify the dead
To look so terrible, so I've studied calm,
Studied quietness till the right time comes
Which gives me calm. I am magic, then:

Magic enough to greet a person from the scraps and bones
Someone risen out of the feast of coals, a person
Fallen through our festering death, but risen up
And singing gladly of her current death.

A Taliessin Answer

What have you been?
A thunderharvest of twinkling grain.
A vivid gang of molten pig-iron.
The great man-eating skull that opens against the sky.
A whistle made from the wingbone of an eagle.

What have you been?
Escape from murder in the posthole.
A door opening on a stairway.
Frankensputin's monster.
The great luminous brain.

What have you been?
A nice meat pie without cartilage.
A wound in air.
The path of least resistance through the water.
The great Christmas reefer passed hand to hand along Hadrian's
   Wall.
The hiss of thick slices of bacon.

What have you been?
The loose shawl of a minister in the wood sitting alone on a
   log.
The subfusc overalls of a lawyer of note: much heated mud is
   flying.
A ladder of smoke on which a spirit climbs to heaven; I pass
   away.

What have you been?
A rain-begetter, a rain-splitter,
I had twenty-three aluminium eyes and long red hair like a
   horse's tail.

I was a frail sea-ear, a shell in the Atlantic fetch, listening;
An octagonal correspondence;
A leech daily regaled on the white rump of a lady of quality.

What have you been?
A pair of little old-fashioned spectacles,
A halo of inextinguishable guilt,
A brown violin on a white altar-stone,
A great vaulted godown, a baisodrome,
An undine-vase and a ghoul-sack,
A pair of enormous eunuchs playing draughts,
A cleft cathedral and a humiliation that suited me,
. . . and I have been foetal hair and an infinitesimal thumb
in a just mouth, a wispy cloud radiating a little above a
town full of children, and a bottle of ash with a green
velvet stopper; I have been a remunerated evil and a cold
tiger, a spayed gunman, a tiny clairvoyant power harmless
and green as a sunny meadow; I have been whirling
lights and spinning discs in a computer where lightning
and mineral submitted to supermarket interrogations;
I have been nearly lost in a pointed brush-stroke that
spread me carefully in lavish papery conversations and
debates among fishwives; and now the moon is filling
like a peepshow with things I have never been; I have
never been tendentious catastrophes, never newspapers,
a psychoanalyst, a pair of ill-matched lovers, not yet.

Which did you love?
When I had a small boy's notion of doing good, when I was
A mirror propped in a garden to repel toads and basilisks.

Tell Me, Doctor

"Dew on dead bodies: big joy"
(*Zolar's Dream Book*) Doctor Solus

What do you make of the petals on the body, doctor?
She grew in the mirror at my back.
The dead body wet with dew made a humped shape
A wide-eyed body strewed with wet petals at the tree's foot
Like severed eyelids, so many eyelids
Shucked off and still we couldn't see. She grew
Old in the mirror, now I watch it empty over my back
And see only blank volumes, wide doors and staring ceilings
An unhealing blank place in the mirror,
And no she at my back. I was surprised at first
To feel my tears, until they grew like roots
Feeding to my mouth for nourishment, the salt taste
And the throbbing breakdown: I was surprised at first
To find my groin stir at the dead wet body
As if it wanted and began to seek out new life.
What do you make of the petals on the body,
Doctor? What of the dew wetting this dead body?
Should we not try to open our eyes under these showering
Dead things, doctor, as we shuck the old body off its back,
This blank place on the ground, as now we brush the petals off
    the face? Brush
The so many eyelids from the sightless face, doctor,
Brush scales off one pair of eyes at least.

The Haunted Armchair

"... and hid his lord's money ..." (Matthew 25)

I want it not to go wrong. I want nothing to go wrong.
I shall guard and hedge and clip to the end of my days
So that nothing goes wrong. This body, this perfect body
That came from my mother's womb undiseased, wholesome,
No, nothing must go wrong. It is not I. It is not I.
No, it is not I. I is lodged in its head's centre,
Its turret, a little towards its eyes; it is not I, it is not I but it
    is mine
And an over-ranking shame to disease it, to let it discase.
I wash my hands, I wash my hands, I wash my hands once,
    twice, thrice,
I rinse my eyes with the sterile saline; I close, I pull the thick
    curtain,
I close the door and lock it, once, twice, thrice, I sit, I lie,
    I sleep in the great armchair,
And I sleep. Sleep, sleep is the preservative, cultivate sleep, it
    keeps me perfect.
No, no, it is not I; I lives only in the turret;
It is the body, it is the body, it is the body is the loved thing,
It is from my mother, it is my mother's
It came from my mother, it is an organ of the body of my
    mother
And I shall keep it with no rough touch upon it
No rough disease to ramp up and down in it. The world?
And the world? That is the mind's. In the turret. And now I
    will sleep.
I will sleep now, for my body exists. That is enough.
Something wakes me. Is it the fire?
It crackles like a speech. The buffet of winds, the cracks
Of the beams, the taste of the sun, the swimming shark of the
    moon?

123

No, I think, no, I think, I think I hear time flowing,
No, I think I hear time eroding, the cinder withering in the
  grate,
The grate withering with the time, my hands raised to my
  eyes
Where my eyes are withering, I look close at my withering
  hands. How long?
How much time have I seen withering? Did I come here today?
Suddenly everything grants me withering. Shall I sit here again?
The body is gone. I sit here alone. A nothing, a virgin
  memory.
A grease-spot. A dirty chair-back.

The Bedside Clock

I. FRIEND ABSENT

The night is fed through the clock,
The day is fed through the clock,
It makes the day black, in columns,
The night a twitching filament,
It is a machine for making
The white black, the black brilliant.
I open the little door at the back
To watch the night go marching in its small machine,
With notched axes nodding in the dark,
And smell of armour-oil.

The world fills up with chains of little knots,
I pillow my head on heaps of quenched sparks,
Wear a shirt of ticking shadows

The night is fed through the clock,
The day is fed through the clock
In the night the stars wheel notched imagination
The day turns black with time and longing

II. FRIEND PRESENT

It sprints up silver stairs with copper heels,
It is a godown piled with ticking copper straw,
There is clock-box going on, repeated rick,
It clanks aloud in choir with each smart tick.
It is a box of crevices and gullied halls
Whose compact orchestra saws the coffined air,
Whose mainspring ebbs in glossy compressed rings,
Whose fringed wheels toss echoes deep and far
Through nimble galleries and scaffoldings,
Whose works assist each other through the steep round night.
It is a clockwork pond, with bronze birds
Plumed with chinks, pecking ratchet fish. . . .
But why do I watch so curiously, and alert? Why,
I and my friend have just been going
Very deeply into the nature of things—look!
Surf of thread seethes round our skins, we draw sheets
With a whisper of blanched manes up to our chins.

The Flight of White Shadows

Over the crooked notice-board crying 'Private',
Over 'Greenlease' one half rented to the weeds

That munch its shivering windows, over the wide flat waters
Streaked by the gulls with long white cries,
Tripling the reed-hiss, killing the reflections,
The brusque shower comes. Each drop binds in itself
A terrestrial globe for nobody's inspection
Incurving sky full of meadow, gravid horse, farm, folk
   focused, each
Splashes itself many times over in leaves,
On rocks, worlds out of worlds, into worlds, before entering
The troubled horsetrough or the lying-down ditch
Still and long, that held a slightly vaster
Version of the sky. It is not a day for reflections,
Not even the smallest, of bird-bath, hoofprint, flowercup,
So slaughtered by swarming lives, the little bombs
Hacking away, whose twinkling self-assassinations
Tumble like consequences; confluences
Threading through tree-towers. A flap of thunder
Shakes out the clouds in the greatest of them all
Who, when in smooth vein, binds the sky into one salt,
One ferociously-curving whole whose theme is high sun
Boring his windy fire-holes—today is roof and ceiling,
Tiles and shattered snowing,
Racing acute edges on to the seashore.

Hordes strike, and forget themselves immediately, are gone
Water into water, or into stone speckling without sympathy,
So what afterlife for the vehemence of sheer-fall,
The blackener of the sky with the limpid on earth,
Spater, bridge-bungler, gouger of fellow-water,
Bruised eggs streaming with a thin vision,
Smashed fruit under black banners? The same, though
Drawn through rock, honeycombs of knives,
Staircases of razors, chasms of scimitars,
Sandy scythe-galleries, division and redivision,
Unlikely rejoinings, green amnesias—all

To the one reflection down river-paths,
Passed down by the rivers, down to that larger,
To the vastation, which is not
The same artist for an instant either.

The Half-Scissors

Humming water holds the high stars.
Meteors fall through the great fat icicles.
Spiders at rest from skinny leg-work
Lean heads forward on shaggy head-laces
All glittering from an askew moon in the sky:
One hinge snapped; a white door dislocated.
The night leans forward on this thin window;
Next door, tattered glass,
Wind twittering on jagged edges.
Doors beat like wings wishing to rise.
I lean forward to this thin fire.
A woman leaves—even the flames grow cool—
She is a one hinge snapped, I am a half-scissors.

Frankenstein in the Forest

"I am afraid for the meat
Of my illegitimate son

127

In the warm autumn.
When will the lightning come?"
Much wisdom had congregated there
In the open-air laboratory which is a cemetery
Under the great oaks
In the litter of acorns:
Mute parcels of impending forests.
There are grim-mouthed toads
Flocked round a boulder of quartz
Deep, complex and prodigious
That gloams in its depths
And twitches there as with a flutter of lightning.
On a portable radio
The size of a hymn-book
A harpsichord plays Scarlatti,
It suffers an attack of amnesia
As the lightning steers near.
The darkness has eaten everything except his face
The alert wise face
Backed by a view of tossing trees,
The bones of his skull
Are as loose as the leaves of the forest,
"I will send lightning through him
It will live under his skin
It will heal his mouldering
Undead bric-à-brac of other men.
There are so many bibles
Without a crack of light;
Mine has pages of slate
With fossils clearly inscribed,
Leather from racehorses
And crocodiles,
Thin frying leaves of electricity
That lies obediently in its place,
Man-skin, oak-bark and quartz. . . ."

The marble grave-stones
Are covered with equations
In the master's quick black analytick crayon,
Their stone books open at only one page;
"It is my great lightning son
Dressed in metal and bark
And the limbs of departed men,
Lightning peers out of his eyes;
He will heal their mouldering.
It is time
To raise him on the sizzling platform."
The lightning makes a blue cave of the forest,
It strikes violently at a hawthorn tree,
A sweet smell fills the air,
It has blossomed heavily.
Now the bright blue
Thistling sparks have stuck to his poles,
His crystal machine
Fills with spangled golden oil.
His golden beehives' buzz rises to a wail
And the monster ascends on its winches,
The clouds draw up their heavy black pews
The rain falls
And the lightning services.

The storm clears.

Cloud-men are digging
Deep blue graves in the sky.
Out of the machine steps
The man, mute, complex and prodigious,
His clothes flickering with electricity,
His first murder not due until tomorrow.

From Love's Journeys

II

In the cathedral if I am not there
those stone whorls, bony girders,
nooks and recesses like the
cancellar galleries of dead bone, they
relax and furl, lap
like the gentlest draperies, the
house of god is a tent
sensitive to his airs, and the other people
are all aware of this and pray
special prayers of a labile
emotional kind in my absence;
stone priests serve at the altar when I open the door,
instantly worship petrifies. I long
to enter the stone world and learn
the secrets of soft hardness, hard softness, like those
the Cheddar caverns know, through millennia
taking their stone photographs of above,
the racing seeding forests, the rising
boneyards of the animals, caught in water
and lime and gentle driblets raising
stalactite patterns of the world above
that petrify me as I enter,
I am so short-lived.

IV

I drink at Glastonbury
from Joseph's well, I pluck
a water-flower in my hands
that springs from the long

coppery-tasting roots of water
winding below the hills and through
the flowers and thorns. The bossed
roofs of the churches repeat it
and the knots
tied at head and feet
of the peaceful likeness of the
reclining stone bishop: much comes
to rest in the water-flower.

VIII

My biologist friend
had many accomplishments, he would
incubate a snake's egg, or the
egg of one of the great fishes
within a test-tube packed
in a great straw box and then
dissect out the small curled
squab or embryo setting it
in its jelly into a special
ring with a small hinged
door and placing this
on his earfinger would
prod said finger into
his head and listen
to the unborn wisdom of
the unconscious snake,
the wide-eyed unliving fish.
He had hair that was
tangled and scurfy, you
could work a radio on so much detail,
and he certainly picked up
useful sayings, such as
you must keep your Teresa alight.

X

Love unites
shock
and permanence
and drink
is a combination
of idiocy
and celibacy, or
so I reflect
crouched at a table
in a Western Region buffet bar
with the sunlight
sliding rapidly through
the train's windows
like notes on a mouthorgan,
like country tunes.

XI

She offered him a blue
thistle-flower, parting the
semen-soft head he found that she
had tucked a white
aspirin into the blue
flock. He pondered
the meaning of her gesture:
she was the anodyne
among the blue sheets; his seed
contained an
anodyne for her
aches; he needed
an anodyne for his
mentality which was too

132

intrusive was it during
intuitive blue intercourse; his
sex needed an aspirin
to stop the nagging; and he
mentioned the matter to
the other woman who said it
was simple: drugs
including drink were of
too excremental a
whiteness.

XII

I did not wish her
to erase the night
not at first but
she sliced such
great holes in beautifully: I
was only inquiring, and we sleep
late into the morning. Instead
of night I have
the blue flash
of a nylon shirt stripped off in the darkness
the sudden
crackle after sleep of radio static
on a blank waveband at morning's four o'clock.

XIII

He is at ease in mud. He
folds it around him
like a great dark
cloak, this is because
he lives in a house
of mischievous children, they have
dim idle hands in the

twilit rooms, he
rebukes them sharply, they weep
tears like rotting icicles, and she
wears a nitrocotton nightdress, she
is sheathed in potential explosions.
But the mud is soft and dark, and will
not, whatever you do to it,
explode, and ablutions
after it are a gross
rewarding priestlike task,
under the lustrous garden hose
enclosed in the starlit glitter.

XIV

When I woke up
I was in bed
with my boots on, and
my wife was nowhere to
be found, I had not
convinced myself
even now of
the innocence and
purity of
her cavities which
I had caused to be
sealed by the
introduction of
contraceptive
devices, so, as I
thought, she would
have leisure to rub
mint into my

beard so that
every thread felt
green and I would have
big eyes like
hanging mirrors and in
each hair of my head
would ramp innumerable
golden lions.

XV

Let us
have all our
divorce-courts floored
in hardish lard, so that
the emotional heat
of her lawyer's plea
sinks him
until he is stifled.
Encourage in these
places cool advocates
with cool heads
and cool limbs signifying
combustible hearts.

XVI

If god had intended
us to run on
all fours he
would have made us
cowards. I wanted a
boat constructed so that
it would melt
in the middle of

135

the pond: *I wanted
to save the lady*. But she
was not bothered, she had
a tongue like a hot
snail and even her
wristwatch was
carnal: I took it
to the jeweller and he
mended it like a man
picking meat from
a lobster-claw.

XX

A great forked tongue
of light licked up
the people streaming into
the Big Top where the
Duchess of Cunt was waiting
to award me my
school prize of sex-
instruction booklets, her
admonishing voice boomed
distantly in the forking
quagmires of my brain
and for the first time
even the headmaster
looked forked under the
black curtain he wore. And
Her Grace's face was
twisted to the left and
beautifully powdered and looked
like a carefully-laundered
sheet badly-ironed waving on
a forked flagstaff.

136

XXI

Pebbles in the wood, people
in the wood, sheep-skulls
in the wood, all
listen to the small rigid
radio-sets the size of
psalters full of
gay laughter, is there any
difference between the full
and empty darkness?

XXII

How well policed the
sky is tonight with
rapid squads, we
shall have rain to
forgive us in the morning.

XXIII

A car moving across the rim of the far cliff like a
gleaming mineral particle detached from the strata.

The cliff below me like a great cannon shooting at the
clouds with the sea.

Below, a white rose swirling in the foam between the
rocks; it runs with brilliant white legs up the stones.

There are big lichened boulders lying sunk in the
upland meadows like rugous starfish awaiting the return
of the sea.

Then rain comes dashing over the sea like the prow of
an immense white ship made of glimmer and mist. It
comes straight at me and I am peppered with harmless
bullets.

After that I felt real in the landscape, the grass settled into grass, the birds moved black as pips in a rectangular pattern in the sky, like a high figure of dots on a blue dice fortunately-fallen. My skin and my eyeskin had been rinsed open by the rain. I felt as though I had been caught up in a whirlwind, and let down again gently, my skin glowing and my hair wet.

The little shabby teahouse was a haven from a lot, though the immense clouds moving rapidly outside were not enemies. They shook gently across the uncurtained window like curds across a blue stone tablet, the soft agreeable to the hard.

XXXI

The summer air outside was
striped with shadows of
grass and trees, we had opened the
window and the tiger stepped over
the sill on to the striped carpet like
suddenly-moving striped air. I had observed
such intrusions before in a spider that
moved fast like crooked shadows or a
universal small crack in things
always running somewhere. Now
we had the tiger and outside the
trees moved in soft
small gestures like a baby's
hands.

XXXIII

Family bible:
stout leather bottle

containing a speckled
white fluid.
Mother insists
the black
bits
are nourishing: I see her still
reading hers
at the kitchen table
grasping a knife
slicing pearly onions
and weeping freely
at the story of how rousingly nourishing
Jezebel was to the palace dogs.

XXXV

Our president rots
in his bedroom, hélas.
It is a once-bright
country. It was. The flags have been
at half-mast for
generations, the wigs
of the
flunkeys are their own
fallen hair. The wombs
are full of
blank faces and blood. Only
underground, far beneath
the exhausted soil the
great rocks still
wing silently.

Dr Faust's Sea-Spiral Spirit

I am frightened. It makes velvet feel too tall.
Its crest peers in at the library window and I cannot open the
    books,
They hug themselves shut like limpets months after it has gone.
The roses have learnt to thunder,
They spread petals like peals of red thunder echoing,
The sky looks like blue boxes of white powder being smashed
    by grey fists.
God is an angel in an angel, and a stone in a stone,
But everything enters this, and is gone.
That cry makes everything look afraid
And how small a whisper do we hear of him
Merely the brushing of his outer garment.

It passes pallidly over the meadow
And suddenly it is brilliant with pollen
It will now seek out female fields of flowers
It cannot help that, they will draw him.
It will pass through a field of bulls
And every hair will be stripped
And every bone broken
But the seed will spin on
A column of translucent horn pulled to the cows
Its seething tip.
It will so use a city
For the sake of one woman.

It destroyed an archipelago.
It was selecting human organs and a dhoti.
It reverses direction and is a person
For I have spoken to him, and he inhales deeply
And thinks deeply, and he speaks and he ceases speaking

Then there is an unforgettable perfume on the air
The woman to fit which I will seek for ever,
And an unforgettable tune for her to walk to.

That cry makes everything look afraid.
The bones float up to the ceiling and the iron bar bends.
It strips a whale for its immense bones
And stands the empty meat on its tail.
The rapid alteration of perfumes in it
Will kill with alternation of memories.
It is a shop of carpets furling and unfurling.
The plain pinafores alert themselves
And are a hive of angry spots.
It is a house of wineglasses and towering butter and cabbages
And its scream is the cry of wool under torment
Or a silk scream, and it is constructed like buttons
And I cannot hear what he is saying
For the wool-and-bone
Screaming at me of his buttons.
Yet the practised shaman
Drums until it appears,
Runs up its sides and travels the whole earth over,
Pees over its crown, a magical act
It is his glass ladder to heaven, his magical cannon
That can be fired once only, what nonsense!
Master Alice descended it, inspecting the good things
Arrayed on its shelves, it may also be summoned
By wounding the air upwards
With a rifle, or by burning Dresden
(There it was seen spinning between
Ranks of buildings gustily burning,
Casting light from winged chevrons), or
By laying the Tarot in an anti-clockwise pattern.
I suspect it and its wife are responsible for Moses' head
And the ten great transmissions whose echoes never stop

Piped along the pair of them hurt my head too
Among all the others.
It will also let down as on a four-cornered cloth
Ancient gifts and treasures, such as
A whole slum of Ambergris like a
Giant's pock-marked skull in curly earwax.

God was found with his head poxed to the bone
He had walked through a hungry cloud of it
It is everywhere it is one and many
It is ships of the desert-seas that sail fleets of it
It stands in linked chains on a calm among icebergs
It is playing its enormous chess and takes a berg with one of
    itself
Crashing a boom, and it takes each other
With a twang like a bridge breaking,
At Christmas dinner I have cracked it
Out of the brown dust of a walnut and as the bathwater runs
    out
It tickles my toes, it is manifold behind the iron doors
Of the neglected casemate, swinging
And breathing in restless thickets,
They say space is sewn of it and I have seen it pouring through
    the telescope
There it is at the north pole shining with the moon
And with the midnight sun, go to the south pole you will find
    it there too,
And between them they keep us all spinning
Growing so tall their crests freeze and throw off
Ice-circlets sparkling, flying diadem upon diadem
Called UFO by the observers, scrutinizing our latitudes.
And yet I have known it
Stand still at my right hand long enough
I have opened the little cupboard in its flank
And plucked out the small brown monkey who lives there

Who became my friend and stayed with me a good while.
It wrenched itself from the head, and the head listened with its
    lack,
It wrenched itself from the rock, and the snail crept in its wake.
To Red Indians it always carries a dead spider gently in its
    buzzing jaws
As the refugee mother carries her dead baby many miles in the
    dusk.
The anatomist tells me I have a pair of small idols of it set in
    my head
That are the kernel of hearing: the tone-deaf apparition
Is a river on tiptoe, rhythmically digesting its own bed.
But it is also a band of eyes and a solid wall of God
Seeking embrace, and it is the great one from the North
That opens like theatre-curtains and there are four beasts
    marching
With a man on a throne inside, but I know too
That it sets with a click and leaves skimming on the waves
The great pearly nautilus that lets out its sails and scuds gently
    off
Its inhabitant glowing dimly through the thin shell walls
A coil of luminous foam by night and a swimming red bone by
    day.
Thus it seems to me. To itself
It is trees, with high leafy galleries
And scrolls of steel, equation-shaped; a man, bearded,
Strolls up its staircase, a bird
Alights on its branches. With our spiral stairs
We have built it homage, it mounts itself in homage
To its own perfected double helix; that crucifix
Dangling between your breasts is a long-section of it.

Like the unicorn's horn it is male and female at once
And emits waves of all lengths from intense internal friction,
It will make a white sound on your transistor

Though a few notes of church organ might fly together:
Chance will have it so among all the other sounds;
And the electricity that branches through its lacquered walls
Is of a purer fine than armature-power, that whining sham;
You can time a great clock on its global pulse.
It is the pouring tower of pebbles
That walks the coast glittering in the cool evening,
It is trees among trees that are trees
Until it decides to leave the forest by revolution.

But men have pinned the giant down in clocks and churches
I watch its face wounded hour after hour
Behind the glass of my bedside clock,
Hacked into numbers, plucked
By enumerating metal
Welded inside a castle:
Within its fortress-windows rounded axes
Powered by its replica in metal
Chink like milled money
Fiscal time
But I would love to go the church
And be served by its priest
In whirling petticoats
Where the Host
Greasy with electricities
Flies into our mouths
Like flocks of roasted pigeons.
It changes places
With Job continually.
It carries seven directions in itself
And five elements,
Music, and thunder,
And small gods laughing with patient happiness.

Slice it low down and find a fish

Lower still, granite and chrysoprase
Fairly high, the embryo babe in water
Higher still, his wail winds out of the wound
He travels at youth-speeds
In the slimmer reaches
Moves zodiac-slow with beards
Through the greater girths.
I take a sip
From the cup chained to its waist.
Faust shunted himself.
Indeed he tamed it
Peered through the sea in it
Inspected the mountain for gems.
I saw him bounding over the Carpathians
Like a child on a pogo-stick.
To cheat the devil he was interred in it four hundred years.
Its grip over the land has eased.
Warm summer breezes
Flow from its palm
Faust strolls happily
Through its flowering palms.
At the bow, the atom; at the stern, the zodiac.

The atomic bomb is a bad picture of it, clumsy and without
    versatility,
It discriminates not at all, and there are too many bad things
    to say about it,
I will not spend time on that figment of the thing I am talking
    about.
It hums like a top and its voice smashes volcanoes,
Yet it will burrow and from the riflings of Etna
Speed skyward, hurtling pillar of red rock.
The mouth is not necessarily a one-way trip
Though you should take plenty of room.
It has shaggy lips, a necklace of pines.

It electrifies Perranporth sand-dunes
Every grain crackles and hums
In flickering organ-notes under
My blue slippered prints.
It is a great traveller and sometimes slips
Up its own back-passage to assuage its terrible wander-lusts.
When men and women embrace
They impersonate it
They are a cone of power
An unbuilt beehive
We two are a brace of them behaving as one
We invaginate, evaginate,
Time stops inside us.

In it the ticking
Of innumerable stolen clocks
Welds to an organ-note.

It is sometimes made of lightning
And at others nothing but magnetism.
It is a kind of knot
Too intricate to undo
Too virile to pull tight.
Untied, a world explodes,
Tied, it winks out.
Or it hovers
Too restless
To untie the human knot.
It is the last trumpet
And the first trumpet.
It fashioned Glastonbury Tor
With helical fingermarks.
The burglar by night bears
Ten small tough patterns of it
Through the polished house,

146

Each one speaks his name.
It is a kind of walking cliff
And a walking well.
The fossil shell and the empty penis
Alike await this wakener.
The Master comes!
He shuts his blue snuff-box
And the wind stops.
He knows how to wind it
With a certain key
That makes the whole home disappear
Inside-out up the chimney;
Knee-deep knee-deep beware
Croaks the frog far inside it.
Its vomited bees float
Coiling down the hillside.
It has much in common
With the round-dance and cyclotron;
It will hover
Over the winding dance on the sand-beach
It will suddenly reverse
The people vanish and all that is left is a shell.
The Master says, learn from this power,
It is strapped to your wrist like an oyster
And allow it to descend into your mouth
And suck you dry
And let it pluck out your eyes
So they can ride on the storm.
Is the shaft weary?
If this shaft is not tired
There is no tiredness anywhere;
If this shaft is tired
Wait for the new world.
Subdue it if you dare.
My master did.

The long thin one enters
The open lid of his cranium,
Screws down his spine,
Sets with a click.
My master wakes,
Gets up and laughs suddenly,
Totters widdershins picking things up
Favouring his left hand
Since this is the northern hemisphere.
And it whirls directly over his head—
Do not look up, it is his hypnotist!
And the sun, that squints through its sun-spots.

It is the best of rainstorms
Since it so mightily collects
And so mightily lets fall.
It has subdued the great sea-worm
Who hangs upright, frothing in its embrace.
Throw a knife into it
You will wound the heel of a grey witch
Who will not bleed, she is made of cobwebs.
It is the spirit of the sealed boulder
It was born of a beach-pebble, and left by a pock,
It is the spirit of the oil-gusher, the black that yellow burns.
It touches the rock, that rock
Speeds up and is petrol for motor-cars:
A spark of its friction catches
The rock is no more in a shuddering flap! But mostly
It buries this rock-spirit until it is needed.
I will call it a magical name in the Linnean system
Vortex macromphalos and I carry on my watchchain
A silky cocoon reminding me of its quiet moments
Of its transformation and presence anywhere:
In the gnat-swarm with smoky feet,
Faltering in spirals; in the tons

148

Of aching black-water-muscle poised over the campus
Peering in through the long library-windows;
In four winds bound round in one breast and breeze.

Dr Faust's receipt for THE NAILS
   Seek out its unfreighted apparition
   It will be a shimmer between oaks at evening
   Celebrated glancingly by gnats
   In broken spirals, falling and rising.
   Anoint with the lizard. It will turn horn-white.
   Now take nails of sweet-tasting iron
   Drive your nail into the floating bone
   Strike it as it returns each time
   Draw sparks with your blows, keep it
   Spinning, persist. The Whirlwind
   Will shrink, measuring gradually
   Its substance into the nail
   That falls to the grass heavily.
   You may use this nail for many benefits.
   Drive it into rock and the hill will be glass,
   You may peruse its secrets.
   Drive it into a table of dry wood
   It will bloom like a bridefeast.
   Drive it into the skull of a blind man
   He will see men like trees walking.

For Julie Kendrick

Pieces for Voices

The Son of My Skin

I

Emperor, Doctor

Emperor: Doctor, how long may a man live after he is flayed?
Doctor: Sir, under proper medical conditions, a man may grow
A whole new skin in a matter of months.
Emperor: Now tell me the most expedient way
Of flaying a man so the skin is unblemished.
Doctor: Sir, there is no way. We would normally begin
With incisions along the spinal column.
Emperor: No, doctor, that will not do.
I must have a skin without blemish
Which is also alive.
You have tissue-culture methods?
Doctor: Certainly the skin can be kept living
Though it would only look authentic if carefully tanned.
I cannot withdraw the living body
Without mutilating incision.
Emperor: That is not true. You have methods
Of plastic surgery that leave no scars. Doctor,
Why do you practise extreme unction?
Doctor: Sir . . . this is not true . . . the priest is called . . .
Emperor: You have a particular drawer in your little black bag
For terminal visits only,

You pack it with ants, and maggots.
You take one of each creature and tweezer it carefully
Into the sick one's hair before taking your leave
Or in his comatose moustache. This is your
Extreme unction, your resignation, and something
Not to be known outside the profession.
You agree?
   Doctor: The people would desert us for the priests.
We need this fragment of magic.
   Emperor: And my sweat. What about that fragment of magic?
   Doctor: Sire, that is true, and secret magic.
   Emperor: I have a distillery of virtues for a skin!
The panels of my skin are the rostas of hospitals.
Male nurses bale up my pillaged collars.
Senior physicians bestow pectoral sweat-bottles.
My work should not include magic.
Naturally I am adept in the magical college,
But I hate every turn, every footfall.
To ascend the ladder of lights
With a face like chewed toffee!
These shamans, they are so noisy!
They stampede us grossly.
The brazier-smoke divests like a stripper,
Garment upon garment unfolding on nobody.
The lean incombustible shaman broods, then bounds to his
   drum,
A grin like a basking toad wings under his long nose,
Maggoty-fingers weaves out the worm-tune,
Whines out of his mouth like a worm-cast crumbling;
Then he chants bloody-muzzles, and with a howl
Battles hobble out of that mouth,
Musketry holes bloom in that voice,
The grimace is a faceful of acid!
The clavicule of a magus is his silent skin.
Then imagination-rhythms crawl through that lantern,

151

The Book of Shadows
Is skin-written each time freshly.
He discovers the pure pentagram by the way his skin shrinks
Like a statue of silk, silent, and tattering;
Sleep clothes and unclothes him with capillary visions.
I am the night-magus,
My skin is the soundless drum,
Still sweat, sprinting sweat, is its tune.
The acts of the surgeons
Beat in advance there, I dream the cure
My sweat is prescription, it is stolen
Greasy with power, clandestine chamberlains
Unwind their bandages through my night-terrors.
My work should not include magic.
I wish to be flayed.
  Doctor: Sire, I could not on my life . . .
You are a man in his prime, in his early sixties,
You have no disease, you are a great prince.
  Emperor: On your life, on your wife's, and your children's,
Flay me.
I must have a skin without blemish
Which is also alive. I want
My living body withdrawn through my mouth.
I want to utter
My new skin and body from the mouth of the old.

II

Rustic Visitor

I have been to the city and seen
A marvellous thing. Our new king
Is a man of pearl, a translucent man.
I saw him enthroned, wearing a gold crown.
Water streamed over all his body

And over his closed eyes from under his crown
With his unshod feet in bolsters of foam
(And he, of all men, is naked)
In a golden conduit from which taps fill vases
And multitudes drink. Priestly men
Hand us water to drink from copper vases
That is slightly bitter and salt
And my sight cleared
After tasting that drink. He sits
Like a man-shaped pearl in a golden round
And the many who minister were all doctors once
Ordained now as priests. There is another man
In a simple robe to whom great honour is paid
They call him "The Son of the Emperor"
And his face is unlined and his arms are smooth
Though his expression says
He is a man in his prime. I have never felt
Such feelings or seen such sights: the golden crown
And the pouring water, the pearl man
Shut in a cone of winding water, eyes tightly closed
And lips pursed as in great concentration
And multitudes drinking.

from
Beyond the Eyelids

Peter Krespel, Jacoba

. . . like thin-skinned insects, which, as we watch the restless play of their muscles, seem to be misshapen . . .

Jacoba: . . . That bird,
           Can you search for it in your head
           Where did it fly to?
Peter: Where it perched
           There's a door in the battlements.
Jacoba: Open the door.
Peter: A twisting cupboard that reaches
           Far back in the wall, stacked
           With thin sheets like mica.
Jacoba: Pull a piece out, hold it in your hands.
Peter: It glides and glistens in my hands. It is curtains
           Over a wall-safe.
Jacoba: Where's the key?
Peter: On the parapet, a great key
           Like a peacock of meat and steel.
           It is so heavy!
Jacoba: Turn the key.
Peter: The earth opens.
Jacoba: Look down inside.
Peter: I lift my lamp.
           It is a winding shell,
           Light glistens round me
           Spirals down, twists
           To a shadowy cusp.
Jacoba: Tread the dwindling stair.
Peter: I push through the tip

Into a glass room
Fire hangs at its centre
I peer through the glass
At a curtained room
I see us there.
You say *look down inside*
And I watch from the lamp
You say *where's the key*
And I watch from the newsmaze,
The folded plantations of print
You say *pull a piece out*
I watch from your lap
You say *where it perched*
I'm in the lace of your cuffs
I watch from the eyelets
I fly up with your hand
You say *precipice-fingered*
I cross a hair long as a river
You say *you hit me*
I squat in a sandy tear-duct
You say *a blow to the eyes*
I sit in them
Like mica watch-towers
You say *skulls again*
I slide down your nostrils
I spread through your bones
You say *randy*
I am between
Your slippery skins like eiderdowns
On tiptoe and working your mouth:
Randy, randy, the cider makes me randy
Like your fidgety mirror, Peter, the greedy jigsaw
Where everything fits, the flinching reservoir
Where water won't rest,
A sledding of lids

> *All of them mirrors*
> *Plumed waves wind-scorched*
> *With rags of you burning like chiffon foam.*

Jacoba: Peter, stop it. That's frightening,
You're frightened . . .

Peter: Say something I didn't make you say, like
Greedy love, I love you,
Your mirror-lined lids—
Grow still, don't flinch,
Let the mirror empty.

Jacoba: Made of stalactite water
The lady in the cavern
Weeps thin lids of stone
Gushes fresh fingernails
Lays new bones down.

from

The Jesus Apparition

An Easter Cantata

Georgina and Silas; Jacey; Maxine and Mortimer

Hell's stones speak aloud as they burn bright for an instant
under the passage of God's shining feet

from I. DUET: GEORGINA AND SILAS

Georgina: Here's the path through the wood to the bathing-
place with the ruined boathouse, and the tide's down

over the mud, with the sunset on fire in it. All the blacks and heavy browns have gone, its flanks are purple and blue like electricity, with emerald clefts in chilly satin channels, like silks and velours spun out of earth, laid down by the water. The smell! It's thriving: yeast, and ploughed earth.

Silas: Apples warm and flecked with sunset-blood, the thick turf
Thudding with apples, a chill through the orchard.
There's a storm coming, it's getting dark too quickly,
A sudden smell of sea through the trees,
Thunder blooms behind them.
Lightning!
Lightning's going to bite, it's going to hit
And where it bites it white-blacks you.
It's going to hit and where it hits it commits surgery!
The shore is cold and pebbly in the rain.
The apples are cold and hard swinging in the storm.
The footmarks on the broad sheets of wet sand fade.
The tide is rising, the black rain is filling the cold sea up.
I am inside the cold cathedral of the rain,
The cold cathedral of the stone. Black.
The red snow drifts down deep and goes out in the frigid black.

Georgina: The sun drops too fast   the mud slams shut
the rooks rise cawing   they are sluicegates of
night cascading night   shadows through the trees
are coming at me again   am I screaming or is it the
black sun coming back it has rays of vitriol it is so hot
so brightly dark and sharp oh   but   the black
sun strikes down   in mercy   and fuses me into
the centre of a hot black rock

II. SOLO: JACEY EATING PLUMS

So many souls. Like all the pebbles breeding from all the world's shores. They say a star has been born for every death since the beginning of time: astronomers have worked out the actual numbers. A little girl once told me what happens to people when they die. "They turn into mountains," she said.

Why not pebbles? Or dust. How do you know what's inside a rock? Or inside the hill across the estuary from my front door, where the scattered dwellings look more like well-heads than houses. Or in the holy boulder at Zennor that makes the woman a witch who climbs on it at midnight? Does it have a secret nightfall of stars in there? Or solid light? There is a legend about the standing stones of Stonehenge that, one night a year, doors open in them. In that instant they light the plains with sweeping rays. Then the great stone valves rumble shut again, until the next time. Perhaps all pebbles and stones, mountains and dust are like this. Then on the right evening you might catch sudden grass-growth of light undulating over the beach and under the waves, or at home the sparkle over a dusty table-top, as the infinitesimal city opens its lighted doors.

But I don't believe it. I think stones are hardened people. I think a pebble drops from the corpse when it's carried away. I think there's a little dead scene in this pebble. We hold it a while in a hand or warm it a moment with a bare footfall and it lights up, deep inside. The scene begins to move. A woman shuddering for fear of soil, a man whose dark love has caused another's death, a lunatic still in her cell, a man falling through clouds of anaesthetic in an operating-theatre. They feel again, and as our life warms their stone skins, they move through what might have been. Then we walk on, we toss the pebble away, and all fades. Turned back to stone. Or a few grains of sand.

But I think too of the stones of soft fruit, warmed in the eater's mouth, the small filament inside twitching alight, spat out, maybe on shingle to die, maybe on wet soil, the spike of it rending its own stone portals.

from III. DUET: MAXINE AND MORTIMER

Maxine: Oh, God has just now made me paper-thin. I am shut inside great-grandfather's big black bible. I am a bookmark. I mark the story of the rending of Jesus' clothes. And I mark the story of the rending of the veil of the temple.

Mortimer: And I am through! I rend the thunderclouds, falling, and they are above me, storm-rafters. The lightning darts, and pauses, looking around itself with solid winding light. I see the sudden-lighted world rushing towards me. Then it stops with a jerk. My parachute stops it with a jerk. And revolves it, slowly. I turn myself, I tilt myself like pouring myself, and I am emerging downwards into all the world, and gravity co-operates, and I have control. Still the light builds crooked towers of itself. It lights me understanding. I see the world, the sights are all laid out before me for my inspection, I am about to be of them. Ah! the light leaps between thresholds of purple. The air is swift and safe against me. The wind rises. I am speeding. I am the white airthing racing through the purple thunderdrome, there are no other skyracers in the big air.

Maxine: And I am this thin bookmark shut in the big bible. And I mark the story of the great earthquake, and how the stone of the sepulchre was rolled away and the angel of the lord came and his countenance was like lightning and his raiment white as snow and he said, Fear not ye; for I know that ye seek Jesus which was crucified. He is not here for he is risen, as he said. Come see the place where the lord lay. And go quickly and tell his disciples that he is risen from the dead and behold he goeth before you into Galilee; there shall ye see him; lo I have told you and they departed from the sepulchre with fear

Mortimer: The clouds are winning   they are below my feet   purple   they are above my head   purple   they close on me like a mouth   purple   I am in a stomach of purple its rainfall is dancing formication   I am shuddering out of the harness that keeps me in this darkness and I hold for a moment by one hand and I drop

Maxine: and they departed from the sepulchre with FEAR and they denied the sepulchre with GREAT JOY and they departed with great FEARJOY who had come along to depose them and GREAT FEAR imposed mountainous littleness and their JOY WAS GREAT AGONY and they left running and they left falling

Mortimer: through whistling darkness when will the earth strike me so that I do not always feel this falling darkness

Maxine: and they ran into the sepulchre as had been foretold and they closed the great stone and they closed their great stone and as they closed their great stone   the   light   went
  out

from

In the Country of the Skin

A RADIO SCRIPT

Appearing in this excerpt: Silas (who is also Jonas); Teresa, his black wife; and Tomas (a psychiatrist who is treating Silas).

(*piano plays, out of tune*)

Silas: The dawn resembles a beautifully-tuned piano made entirely of sea-shells. It goes ping-a-tunk with acrid notes as the mother o' pearl keys strike. At the aperture, wreathed with true lovers' knots and other cats-cradles, instead of the sun, our ancestors appear. They are not memories and I never dream.

Teresa: This is what I see also between the toast and marmalade and its shadow.

Silas: You look oddly crumpled as you play, Teresa, and there is a fly walking over your eye. Pay her with tissuey money and let's go.

Teresa: That tune of mine in the cold street has opened up the tightly-wadded ancestor-files, alas.

Silas: The clouds fill up with inherited faces and you've got the shopping to do.

Teresa: The spectacle wins. The faces above are tearing themselves gently to bits that flutter to the street and line the boughs with white. Look, I am covered with your grandfather's white aunts!

Jonas: Well now, God has unleashed his archives and perhaps we can learn something.

Silas: The pages shrivel on my palm as I bend to read.

Teresa: Outstare the snow; let the watery white pages melt on your warm eyes.

Silas: We're in love. We must be. White snowball in your black hand. No snowballing!

Teresa: Look into my snowball. Whose name do you see?

Silas: J–O–N–A–S.

Teresa: Jonas is million upon million of layered micropages. He is the preoccupied snowman, a white pain with coal eyes and an old hat, and he is grateful to Spring for wasting all his contemplation and turning him into simple wriggling water.

Silas: His flakes themselves are so silvery, like Hello, like the first words of our meeting. Greed kills them. He and I are the white door.

Teresa: You are the white door.

Silas: I am the white door. You are the black door.

Teresa: I am the black door.

(*music*)
(*pause*)

161

Tomas: Hypnomania and folie à deux! And mud-fetishism. I've never had a mud-fetish before!

Silas: Haunt me with erosion, Teresa. You are the black door. You broke free from my arm and jumped down into the mud, and lay in it at your ease, like an odalisque, among its cushions.

Teresa: Darkness like mine falls from every pebble. My rocks rot in the clear rain. I was rock, I shall be rock again, but now I am too endlessly deep and soft for thought. I am making endless soil and ponderous thick earth to wander through, I reflect in my wet estuaries. I recline at ease among emerald flanks and winding satin clefts, you will find me in places where clean ladies don't go, one finger up your tail. You look out of your window and see me playing with the dustbins. I look up and see you and smile and wave and smear tea-leaves down my white skirt. I wade the estuaries, I shin down cliffs of mud, I wander through myself, barbaric mire gloats everywhere.

Silas: Now tell me the one about the Lady who Walks . . .

Teresa: That very dirty black lady allows herself on certain occasions to be picked clean by the flies, her numerous allies. They busy themselves about her, they hum high—I am carrying earth in my rostrum for her! For her! Slender midges like eyelashes, even with their soft mouthparts, are glad to manage a grain, a strand of mucus, a thread of waterweed popping with animalculae. The big blowfly bluebottle gobbles it off, crawling pugnose; she is winkling with wings like a blue-sequined skin; then she steps forward out of this ink-cloud her face shining black that can never be white, her dress as radiantly white as when she first stepped into the great mud.

Silas: More, Teresa, more.

Teresa: They come when she needs them. She is mistress of flesh-flies. When she's dirty she can be clean and when she's clean she can be as dirty as she pleases.

Silas: Yes, yes.

162

Teresa: How she loves being dirty and how she loves to be clean! And on gold-veined wings, on brass and fleshy pinions, with her small brawny flies in their jointed horny vestments, her frail grass-green ones, her shiny-bun insects, she can replace the earth grain by grain into the place where it came from, as if she had never wallowed in it.

Silas: More, Teresa, please.

Teresa: But she may let the earth-dirt be, upon her person, for day upon day of her progress, and then in the creases of her dress and through her mud-clotted hair and in the grimy turban wound round her hair the small green things begin to grow, the stubbles and fringes of green and the small beards of moss and weed. Now she is a black lady of green grass and ivy . . .

Silas: Yes, Teresa.

Teresa: And now you have been tied to a lamppost by the Army and you have been tarred and feathered.

Silas: Oh, Oh! (*He comes*)

(*music climax, and out*)
(*pause*)

Tomas: I knew what all that meant, of course. You must remember that her name, Teresa, means "earth". I saw the trouble at once. It was his Will, that he called Jonas, that he called Magick, that was making them both sick and mad. Right at the beginning there were plain signs of the crumbling of Jonas; Teresa's ascendancy was growing. I was engaged to cure Silas of Jonas. I have done so, since now he submits to Teresa. Submitting to Jesus was the old way. Now we say: Submit to the Anima.

We teach the woman what she is. Jonas began this, and encompassed his own destruction. We teach the woman what she is, and we say: submit to the Anima that she is. What this is likely to do to Teresa, I don't know. It's not my concern.

163

Silas, submit to the Anima. Teresa, what does *your* dream say?

Teresa: She is the silver, fish-tailed dancer of the sand.

Tomas: Nothing more?

Teresa: Nothing more.

Nothing more emerges from the dream. The sage sits silently, chewing his finger.

Tomas: There are dreams and dreams . . .

(*music*)

Teresa: The moonlight slowly penetrates him, he is nearly gone. Quick! I am grabbing an arm, it feels pulpy. Quick! Tell him a dream.

So I pull my lids down and pretend to fall asleep and I talk in my sleep about the Anima. Colours flow back into the old freckled body. The eyes open wide and begin to twinkle. He salivates with interest. The white hair over the collar resembles steam escaping from under the lid of a pot. The eyes blaze. The sun shines from the glass skull. My closed black face slowly twists towards his sunlit words and my mouth opens wide as if drinking them.

Tomas: I have cured you, now I must withdraw. Help me up.

Teresa: My dream said: Submit to the Anima. On rising to his feet, he was no longer the saint. He looked down at himself, the realisation of what had happened fading with that which knew it in him. Submit to the Anima. He was a man for whom the morning jug or pail was a friend, the collie in the corner shop. The convicted murderer who visited him under guard was especially a friend. He lived the life of a saint and a healer, but, truly, he thought himself mad. What is this, he said to himself, when every little thing, a grain of dust in a walnut shell, a seaside tavern, looks at me with a countenance, with a face of such friendly openness that I have to cry out "Goodday friend!" Or with a look of such suffering that I must either run past it or kneel and embrace it. And the

164

people! Every wrinkle, every quiver, is a sentence that changes and writes a fresh meaning every second and then declares itself anew. And he stands fast among those hurrying congregations of meaning and he says:

Tomas: I'm mad, I think. Please, can you help me?

Teresa: Sometimes they could. Far too many could never hear his meaning.

Everybody he treats is faced with the question:

Tomas: Have you the cure? Have *you* the cure?

Teresa: And the people he treats hand their madness over to him, expound their mad theories of the origin of life or how they have been tricked and betrayed, and he is inspecting it all the time they talk for the least particle of true madness that would cure him of his insanity. So one morning, he sitting on the edge of his bed, warm and open from the expounding of my dream, in the bare room with the patterned wallpaper he conversed with because it looked so miserable, in the room where he listened thriftily and thirstily to the murderer psychoanalysing him, and this cured the murderer, I whispered to him the one tiny grain of true nonsense: (*whispers*)

Submit to the Anima

And he took it up and his mind inspected it and it ran through his fingers like the hot blood and like tendrils and it flowered in his prick and bushed in his eyes and blossomed in his brain and he parted the leaves and he walked out, and walking out he was no longer the saint he had been. And as I watched him go, he was dancing in the chains he couldn't see, all pain gone.

This is how I found a way to cure Tomas, to exile Jonas, and to live in peace with Silas.

Tomas: I have told you how I cured Silas of his great and terrible Will called Jonas. It was one of my greatest cases.

Silas: Teresa, tell me about *that* again. (*music out*)

(*pause*)

165

Silas: Teresa, tell me about the mud again (*music*)
Teresa sings: And in each hair is a fountain
  And beneath each fountain a door
  And through each door a river
  And in each river a tree
  And hanging in each tree a worm
  And round each worm a bracelet
  And in each bracelet a light
  And in each light a horny skull
  And in each skull a wand
  And in each wand a scroll
  And in each scroll a flock of wings
  With a squad of dew in each feather
  And a lover in each dew
  And in the lover a battle
  And in the battle hidden fountains
  Break within each hair.

The Hermaphrodite Album

No Psychiatry without Penalty

His glamour was immense I wanted to be like him
He chained up stones deeply burrowed where he had grasped
them
Or it was the many-socketed skull of Argus saved from
mythology
He took the worried skulls of adults and distilled the souls of
children out of the bone
Hypnotized these inmates to dwell in rows of his own asylums
Where their selves lean on their elbows out of the stone
windows
Waiting to speak agreeing with him in a chorus of socketed
voices.
He handles the skulls of the world like a bucket of beach sand
Where do you want them he asked pouring them from palm
to palm
Here! I pointed to my frail boat where she sat one of the first
corpses
We fed to the wild sea until it spoke the last chapter for a new
monument.

I have saved a skull-lamp of pale spectral honey
It sheds light and a pawing silence it is sweet but helpless and
ghostly
And there is still a mirror made of himself to hunt through

I should never have entered this mirror but his glamour is
    immense.

I admired his shipwrecks
It was my end's beginning

The oak hailed its future about our ears
Water-drops and acorns in the gust
That's gone

Skulls, nothing but skulls on his showing
He demonstrates the snow
Every flake a tiny crystal skull with gritted teeth

The leaves turn their teeth chatter
I watched at her bed by snakelight
A lamp of snakeoil
My light sneaked over black water
I watched by her bed and she never woke
I watched until her skull lay exhausted in the pillow
I wanted her skull for him it was the first of the plague

His boats still gather in sheeted missions
To inspect the sea-mirror to look behind the sea-crucifix
They send themselves out they are unmanned and unwomaned
I wait on the shore in my sleep they may bring her back
But I know they bring up miraculous draughts of skulls
They are his skulls he has worn them all out himself.

Some Books, Some Authors, Some Readers

There is dead wood in this author; open his book and certain pages crumble like rotten wood between covers of bark. Out of so much else scramble boot-shiny beetles, very compact and intent, like the readers it inspires, like the sincere readers of difficult dead books.

This one sloughs off his dead faces. They are the pages of his books. The old gentleman!—meet him now as pink and sweetly-smelling as a freshly-washed baby. A new book gathers in his face as we talk. He adjusts the shade of the club-room lamp so that it shines away from the darkness gathering in his face.

This one specialises in pages that become water as their white crests turn. Thus you can only read on, but there is a sea there containing many curious fish, and whales that move in schools together among their scented milt.

This one travels over sunlit waters in a shiny tin boat. He is very tanned, almost black, and sails with one hand grasping the white mast, but he cannot look down, the water is so bright.

This one writes books you do not read because they read aloud to you. Immersed in the writing, you lounge up to your neck in the talking water, your collar of water high around your neck, your river-robe fast-flowing.

The books of this one are like biting seaside rock. The same word runs straight through to the end.

This one makes books of stinking quicksilver. It is your own face you regard as you read, but the smell is the author's.

Opening the covers of this one's book is like opening a stove that has not been lighted for centuries. But its clinker is thousands of pearls.

How can I evaluate or describe to you the plots of any of

these books, or the information they contain! For I am a lover of books, and this is my misfortune; to tell their worth is beyond me.

Movement

An empty mirror fills up slowly with a black hieroglyph.
The neatly-shaved poodle parades the green lawns:
A piece of wiry writing. Black snow falls,
Little black footprints run over the clean washing.
Ants write a ravenous sentence in the picnic garden.
The spider hitches her web about her on the syllable "snaaaa"
With a silent rattling.
The fly completes with a fat little "aaatch"
Like a black peach.
The mirror empties gradually.
It fills up with a white hieroglyph.
White poodle, white snow, snowmarks invisible on white
    washing,
A dairy-spider and a floury fly,
A white peach with a brown pinch-mark.
Eat it now, or move on.

The Soldier Who Almost Drowned

The soldier who almost drowned
        stumbled on a dry path
        could not quench his thirst
        could not light his cigarette, matches and tobacco
           were sopping
The soldier who almost drowned
        his buttons were always dirty
        his belt-brass black
        solid mud behind the glass of his watch
        pockets full of spirogyra
        his lips gritty
        he feels the currents purling between his teeth
The soldier who almost drowned
        met Meg, who said she'd make a better job of it
        met Sally, who was skinny and caught cold easily
        met Justine, who smelt of wet fish
        drowned himself briefly in Patricia, and went away
The soldier who almost drowned
        posted a lookout, who was gravel-blind
        loved women who dressed in weed-green
        enjoyed the pounding of drums—it made pictures
           of his past life flash in front of him
        admired the bubbling speech of babies
        built glass-bottomed boats
The soldier who almost drowned
        made an income from extracting gold from
           seawater—500,000 gallons yield one ounce
        irrigated Niagara
        gave parties on the frozen Thames
The soldier who almost drowned
        remembers old battles in the rain

the men who splashed mud when he fired at them
the rivers of napalm
the night air solid with monsoon
the burning tank he drove into the boot-polish
    river-water
The soldier who almost drowned
    confessed how the pearly bubbles from his mouth
      flew upward
    how the mud lurched into his boots and trousers
    how his limbs moved with slow delicacy down
      there, a dancing
    how his skin was watery, and rippled
    how the ripple rafters enclosed him above
    how the sun muted acceptably
    how the explosions rang like soft bells
    how his sins became plain to him
    how the river unwound his life
    how he slept on the river-bed, at peace
    how he awoke on the mud-bank in the
      dawn-breeze in disbelief
The soldier who almost drowned
    drank weak tea and ate a lettuce sandwich
    had a chlorotic weak skin
    I saw him raise a finger and it dribbled away
    I called him my friend but his ears were full of
      water
    I saw him drifting away on the tide
    he came to with a jerk and spoke to me
    saying he wished he could come to the sea he was
      always drifting there
The soldier who almost drowned
    had a streaming cold
    drank gallons to stop himself evaporating on the
      golf-course
    I did not see him go

I found a drenched pair of pyjamas in a wet bed
we put these in the coffin and fired our fusillade
   over them
I saluted the clouds rising with the sun that evening
and wept with the dewy moors in the morning.

Brothel Allotment

The house where the smoke from the chimneys is as red as
blood.

The woman in the house who is also the floor: her dress
flows into her long skirt which weaves into the carpet.

The old man in the kitchen who is also the oven.

The young woman of the house who enters from the drains,
wearing green.

The young lad who visits, smelling of grass-cuttings.

The meal of appleseeds served.

The hot petrol drunk.

The stairs that are the keys of the piano that musics them
upstairs.

The bed that is an inlet of the sea.

The covers that are white and salt and the bedlight that goes
down red.

The awakening to gulls and sleet.

The breakfast of loose change.

The street home that is a well.

Erosion

Darkness is a power. She haunts with power.
I begin to fear the pebble and its outpourings, I fear
The blood of the nearby hills, the outpourings
Of the rock. She makes endless soil
And ponderous thick earth earth wanders through,
Presiding from her hills, reflecting herself
In her wet estuaries. She reclines at ease
In emerald flanks and winding satin clefts,
And wanders through herself. Mire gloats everywhere.
The lurching packs of birds
Bear mire-stings in their tails,
They eat her fruit and make more mud.
I admire
The clean acid scut-bite of the enormous wasp.
She was rock, now she is endlessly deep
And too soft for thought:
Too much dark and power to stifle in. Her rocks
Rot the clear rain. Sometimes I see the clouds above the
    shored-up mud
Tugged open as if by the hymns of mud mud sings,
Hymns to the sky out of her low dank softness.
Each night from hedgerows
Huge glossy slugs skim out, hour-long transparencies
With mire-cud inset deep that melts
To individual flesh and back again,
Not like those hills that spend themselves completely,
Leave place slowly in their thick green dresses
To bathe their heads and sink in ever-mud.

Celebration

(GHOST-AUTOPSY)

An altar on a rock;
A cup with a spring of water in it;
A stone made of ox-blood;
A silly old man in a nightie, the celebrant;
The taste of sleep in a lollypop;
A pigsty with antlers nailed above the door;
Winged death, carrying a broken egg;
Twine, needle, corpse.

His silver head nid-nods,
The cup alights on the stone,
A cup with the spring of water in it,
A sundial working up a thirst.
The summer sleeps.
Paradise was beneath the water, and still is.
The ponds are heavy,
A column of gnats weaving above a sundial.
We watch the nightie brandishing the sword

Carving the corpse on the terrace of life.

Lymph full of stars!
Unfolding the cerebral hemispheres—gills!
Behold! the man who brewed me,
The stone full of pearls, the sea-glands.

Uncollected Poems

The Agnostic Visitor

For Roy and Agnes

Dawn, his first day.

Slowly the mountain fills the window.
They are off to the church. They offer him coffee.
Gently enquire how he'll pass his first morning.
"Finish my coffee, browse in a book, take a short stroll."
They hear him out mildly, carry plates from the kitchen,
Lay him knife and fork quietly, with an indwelling look,
God-takers, inlooking, take none for themselves,
Lay him fork and knife quietly, a white folded napkin,
Carry plates to the kitchen. God-partakers
Touch his hand mildly, bid him goodbye.

And on that walk the visitor paused
Looked head up around me snuffing the hill air;
The hill-face opposite across the valley-steep:
Slate racked and slotted like shelves of great books
Leaning tall folios, and the hills bent-shouldered
Like great slow readers crowded around
With their indwelling look, sides trodden by god-lovers
With their indwelling look. And I pulled at the roadside
Tugged down a small slate.

                    Into the rock bed
Clear water gathered, water spilled over
From inside the mountain, long cool water
Threading the mountain within the soft turf
Under the hard rock, falling presence of water
Reaching from peaks, downward and cool,
Moist stone aflow, thick turf-springing.
I plucked my stone down, the socket a freshet,
Dabbled a hand, raised my palm to my lips,
Sipped indwelling water. With an indwelling look
Trod on down the cutting, reading my brief slate,
The mountains following.

Hush! The Sun

A warm tawny street. Houses buried in trees,
Broad hollow sunshafts, leaves plump as fruit,
Bright russet walls. Hush burns from the heat,
You can see it, it spreads,
Great cars draw away, like threads in silk.

Up through our window, hung on this hush,
The silences rise, and we fall quiet.
Green mowers spray a deep whitening hay-hush,
Boys play in the streets, skip and call out.
One trips in a knee a knock down to the quick;
It lets red silence fall like an idling flag.

He is strung on his cry, tongue high in the mouth
Stretched like a mast; his mouth at full gasp
Brimmed with the hush. The air is too thick,

The summer too broad, too easy, too sweet,
It coils down his throat, he hangs crook'd in its honey,
It glints at his lids, he is strung on its flow
Too golden and sunny, too rolling and hazy
For mere blood to shake, too heavy, too lazy.

Great cars draw away, like threads in silk.

Stained-Glass Windows to Suit Every Pocket

I have examined all the rooms of props and I am not satisfied.
I will travel to the card-makers and devise my own pack.
With the Devil's Pasteboards I will make my own portable
  church.
Every man may take his church out of his pocket and play
  patterns with it
Which is to say, pray, meditate, and enter the four suits of his
  own nature.
No priest will own this church and no lands or cottages will
  be owned by it
There will be no squire to act as the church penis jus primae
  noctis
And no schoolmaster to addle boys' pates with latin poets.
There will instead be a church that fits into your pocket made
  of 78
Placards of living stones that are plastic and they may if you
  wish

Become windows that are also doors and hymns sermons and
  sacraments also
Their yoke is light because their knowledge is real

The iron chariots and the steel thrones of Charlemagne and
  the Mafia which are
Privies also and instant getaway secret passages—Props. The
  great prick
Of the King's head that thrusts itself with their aid and that of
  a little
Scented oil into the crown of ice and lightning in full view of
  the Tv cameras—
Props. Battersea Power Station: Props. Education for Industry:
  Props.
Wedding-rings: Props.

Do you wish to dismantle the scenery and walk out on to a
  bare stage
And throw open the great iron doors on to the street—take out
  your cards!
Do you wish to come in out of the venal street into a further
  world
Of harmless murders, flat kings, picturesque confessions and
  engaging knaves—
Take out your cards! Remember they are nothing but a pack
  of cards.

I feel real hands travelling over my real skin as though they
  were laying out cards.

From the Questions to Mary

The Virgin Mary gave birth to Dionysus, who said:
When I have grown my horns I shall begin listening to them.
Meanwhile, Mother, why do you yet give me that blissful
    milk
While I can give you nothing back but these turds
Which we throw among the straw?

No, says Mary calmly, there is no blame.
Make me a turd, my son.

And Dionysus makes Mary a warm little turd scented with his
    body
She holds her white palm out and Dionysus lays his
Egg of earth in the palm of her hand
And she takes the turd and she digs a little hole
In the soft earth of the garden and she lays
The turd therein and she takes a nutmeg
And lays it on top of the turd.

Look, she says, we shall water this spot for a year.

That was March, Dionysus three months old.
By April, a slick green spear through the soil.
May gives it white flowers in foamy tufts,
In the summer bees come with their eternity drone,
By the autumn the tree is Dionysus' height,
It bears fruits of gold and others of silver.

Mary says, did I ever make you feel you had stolen milk?
Her son replies: I used to wonder, before this tree,
What I could ever give that was half so good as what you gave
    me.

The Oracle

"You shall be my partner in fainting"
(Puppet-magician in my 11-year-old son's play)

He is very impressive. I am very impressed by him.
His hair escapes from his collar like white steam boiling from a
    pot.
I don't care if he remembers nothing. I don't care if he is deaf.
He is helping me he has agreed to go the whole way with me.

Depression is withheld knowledge is his theme
Go into the dark bravely

He leaves me in the garden
Into the dark bravely
I am in the seat by the sundial, I am waiting for a beam
Time illuminated in a shaft
A tall-beam, brimming with health-days
It comes
          a precise shadow on the stone clock
I rise and look at the time VII on a sunny winter evening
It is a time that reaches into the past and this clock never stops
It resembles time written with fast ink on parchment
It is horoscope time it gives me hope

Behind me the shadows are assembling
I am their hustings and they are holding an election
They are the shadow-party in opposition
The sun's platform has fallen vacant they are unopposed
The shadow-ministers propose an increase in taxes
I remove my jacket and throw it into the shadows
They impose an additional surcharge
I give them my tie

There are further concealed duties and taxes
Where I am going there is no need for shirt and trousers
I shall walk like Adam through the pinewoods until it is time
    to die
And the dew fall on me and the dew fall on me
I sigh and turn away from the sunny hours
Away from the garden sundial along the shadowy path
The shadow cabinet is waiting for me
With opening doors with open arms
They bear me away I burn in the dark I go bravely
Like a wisp of black hair a white cinder
A voice bravely

Part of the dark offers me a black book I had better not say no
His dark eyes flash like rains falling expecting dark pages I open
    the book
I am right the pages are black but the writing is moonlike
The moon is writing on wavelets, the endless nibs busy
I am on the cold black sand reclothed I am cold
I peer over the water trying to read the moon's script
Downy bones in the mist can that be me? If the wind blows
My bones fall to the sand, my bones rise as the water elects
Wavelet flesh of slow water, a gathering-place for mists

The dark story of the child

The blood-tides and your mother rides with all womankind . . .
The moon writes a sudden picture of a woman in a silver boat
A silver woman and the blood sea is ceaseless pulsing

The sundial in the seagarden shows me a moontime V
I look back over the black book of the waves
I have read some of its writing

I know how to faint how to wake how to be written on a little.

A Philosophy in Welshese

The summer before last I saw my vision
Driving back from the cinema along the Pwllheli road
Having consumed no more than a quarter of Welsh whiskey
Glancing out of my driver's window to the right

There was the vision walking over the sea
In a cloud of fire like raw tissues of flesh
Like an emperor bleeding at every pore because he is so alive.
On my left the sun westered behind the mountains
Which were dark and packed with too much scree,
Too many pebbles in slopes like millions of people

But on my right hand you walked over the sea in your single
    scarlet garment!

I searched in my head for what you were called and I shouted
    silently
OSIRIS or some such name and you wheeled slowly
Bowing to acknowledge my cry then as the road turned inland
The mountain got up slowly and laid along the crisp shore
Its pattern of farmers' fields that fitted each other endlessly.

Once there was this Chinese philosopher driving his horse and
    cart
Through the mountain passes and he was not thinking exactly of
    philosophy
His one thought was fuck the slut as he drove carefully along
    the road towards her
Which concept alerted a nearby cloud that was coloured
    exquisitely
Like blood washing away on a cool stream. The same cloud
Had been appearing nightly at this spot for six million years

Pondering over the pass in the ancient mountains without
 hearing philosophy
Expressed with quite such concision and determination before.

Brother! Old Friend! Colleague! I shouted to China.

This cloud rolled down the mountain like an immense glowing
 dog
Followed him home and all night wrapped his house
As all night he fucked the slut and every night
People of the area observed that the sunset descended
To attend this holy man whom the gods kept safe.
He never understood why his reputation grew but he kept hard
 at it
Preaching that if you wish to be loved by men of discernment
Find a slut and fuck her deep as she will go into her yin
Indulging your manifold perversions which you must woo as a
 fair person
Which is what the Welsh whiskey showed me and I wonder
 whether it's true
On the road to Pwllheli driving back from the cinema at
 Bangor
Through the great mountains on no more than a quarter bottle
 taken
With Dante Alighieri, Charles Lutwidge Dodgson and Albert
 Einstein in the back of the car.

Nine Sorceries

(For E.W.W.)

I have no presentation gold watch
That goes green in summer,
Nor cabin-trunk
Like a scooped oak-tree
Hasped with ivy and galls
Under any staircase
And it contains no country moss-folds
Convoluted like brain-fields
With no fresh spring
Easing under hasps
For any talking snake
To sip the frigid water;
I have no flat horn on my wall
For calling up spirits
Made from no great spider
To blow any long tune
Cold as gossamer
Cold as a starlane
From a mouthpiece
Of beards and clockwork;
And I am no kind of bear in winter
Whose breath condenses
Into little cold models
Of the many girls
I have not eaten;
I do not cause the thunder
That is casting
One of its many bristling skins
Outside at this moment;

I do not make the lightning
By rapidly opening
This book, or another;
I do not keep thunder
In these old boots.
But I have been cold
All evening without you
And my watch is slow
It counts yesterday.

This Cornish Passage

The stone church whitewashed for navigation.
These terrible seas. The tall church trees
Spurting rooks like fountains of the dead,
The gorge leaning towards the shore and the boulders
Great as giants' heads, great as their bolsters,
Great as their white beds, towards the sailing vessels.

This mouth, with a white church in it.
The yarrows bend, and weave themselves into odours.
The beetles' furniture of fretted lichen.
Dove-grey tombs, a soft wind.
These dead wrecked in their churchyard, all around.

The gossamer like breathing ladders of glass.

Sam's Call

(For Derek Toyne)

My uncle Sam Lines always seemed
an enlightened person to me, but then I
was a child. I never went
to chapel where he preached, though people told me
he was a marvellous preacher. I asked him what he said:
he told me he never could remember.

He saw his double in the garden. Came in to my aunt:
I just saw a funny chap, an old un under the trees, he said.
All right, said my aunt. Went up to him
to take a closer look and it was me.

He had a lovely death. My aunt told me.
Almost gone, then up he sat, bolt upright and cried:
Meg lass, get me a clean shirt, I'll not be seen
dead in this one. They got him one,
struggled him into it, he never spoke again.

That was when I was guided, the one and only time.
Sam was laid out and waiting for his funeral.
I felt suddenly curious about an old box in the barn
Meg had said was full of old writings, now I must see them.
I went out quietly because of the death in the house
and the blinds down into the barn-smell
of chicken-shit and damp feed. Inside the box I found
one old piece of paper with green writing
"To be buried with Sam Lines," folded,
a red mark and something stuck round and crinkled,
like an ancient condom, then the tears

spurted into my hand, I understood
it was his caul he had been born with.

He could tell the time without looking at his watch.
He'd sleep in his chair by the range; after supper
we kids'd creep up, whisper in his ear,
(head back and closed eyes fixed on the ceiling)
"Sam, what's the time?" His big oakapple hand
crept into his waistcoat head still asleep,
He took his turnip watch out and said the time
from his sleeping mouth. He was always right
you could check him from the watch his big hand
would close and tuck away into its pocket again.

Dune-Firer

Rocked with laughter, he is a Cornishman,
He says: "There are no ghosts in England",
Sand in the gold honey to chip your teeth on,
By the slipping sandhills, in his cottage window
Chewing his pipe, in his shirtsleeves, regarding
The crucifix of day and night, the beehives,
The bees buzzing, and the silent honey,
The painted signboard of the pub that shows
A man with flaming-torch-in-hand
Thrusting his light down a street that's sanded up.

Two stone benches in the church-porch
Two men opposite each other, dozing.
A gargoyle grips the full moon in its jaws.

He uncorked the Shrub bottle and poured me out
A cat's labyrinth of odours pacing round the garden,
A scent like a procession of scarlet judges
Their eyes closed.
                    "The Figure
Of the Saviour broke all the crosses.
Till my Grand-dad came with that stone
Or bone, you couldn't get a crucifix to hang.
The story has it they killed the saint
And his mother on the north beach
Where they were washed up in their tun-cask
At night, and light poured between the staves.
Greatly fearing they crept along the beams
Dazzled by the contents raised an axe
A voice cried—hold! and the iron bands
Sprang off with a chime and the barrel opened
Like a wooden flower, and sitting at its centre
Like stamens, pistil, the saint on his mother's lap,
Her golden breast spilling out of her gown
And he smiling up at them from his white meal.
And they smiled and laughed at the axe raised again
And the laughter went on as it fell splitting them,
And the light went out and the beach bubbled with blood.
The tide glowed and boiled as it washed the floor
So they said it must have been the devil.
And the axe was possessed with holy fear
And did it of itself. They say
That's how the stone was made
As lightning strikes the dunes and fuses sand
Their blood leapt like lightning around the beach.
One of my stubborn fathers cupboarded it in his cottage.
After that the Figure broke all his crosses.
Nothing went right until the bone came to the church.
You saw the figure on the signboard.
That was my Grand-dad in the village street.

The dunes were winning and he'd pulled that bone out,
The sand sprang and sprayed back before it,
The bone sang and the sand leapt back,
Something yelped and sprang into the sea
With a cliff of water as it plunged
And he walked straight up the churchyard-path
And the head-stones rocked and the coffins
Cracked underground like the resurrection
And he marched into the porch and put it up
On the shelf where it lies now, and they made
A little grilled door to keep it safe
And two men on duty all the time . . .

I think it's a bone out of a lizard's back
That walked the dunes two million years ago
And it's so peaceful with its years, it cures.
I've touched it to open-sores, and they scream
Like mouths, and having screamed
They close their lips for ever . . . I've had crab-lice
Run shrieking through the hair until they died.
The men like sitting there, because they dream
Great dreams they can remember, that are the bone's dreams,
Or their own dreams rising from the well of time-stillness
The bone makes in that porch, you'll feel it."
We went through the church, past
Jesus hanging by his wounds in a blue sea-window
Over the altar; a side-window showed how
His head glowed like a thin gold cup
Under his halo as he wondered at his hand-wounds.
My friend nodded to his dozing mates,
Unlocked an iron grille in an inner pillar
Brought out the bone and touched it
To my tongue, I saw the scrotum delicately whorled,
The stout shaft resting, balls caught up in their skin,
I kissed the stone phallus, and he shut it away.

I wanted to ask him what he saw it as,
He thought it was a vertebra, a bit of a backbone,
But I saw it clearly . . . so did he . . .
And I felt the ulcer itching as it healed, I wanted to thank
But he interrupted: "You're not finished.
It's cured your mouth. You'll not be finished
Till you come to guard here as well,
Not till you tear up your books
And come to read here with us in this porch
The book of dreams opened to us nightly,
The living book of scenes fresh-written nightly."

Transform Or Perish

Recently I officiated at the burial of a dead child, a little girl. The child's mother, a young woman, insisted on filling the corpse's mouth with tiny glass beads, piercing the hands with needles, placing a fertile hen's egg in the crotch, and painting the forehead with a dab of menstrual blood.

—And did you permit this?

—Indeed I did. It would have been cruel to refuse.

It seemed to his interlocutor that the scenery of the priest's face had shifted somewhat.

—I was obliged for the first time to have lights in the pulpit. I noted a rent in my robe as I mounted Coward's Castle. I had to speak to Hannah about it. She is—I believe—growing lazy. I wonder if it can be the quietness of our country round. I have my ministry and she has her correspondence. She is growing lazy and I am growing ill.

—I am very sorry to hear it.

—Every time I preach, every time I visit a sick person, I feel what I used to call God's Word, I used to call it the Jesus in me, I feel this something leave me. If I do not allow it to go out when it is called up by my ministry, then I feel that I have locked an innocent and good person into a prison. Yet when it is out of me, I am a husk, I have no force.

The priest held his hand, pale as fishbones, towards the candle-flame.

—In former times God's Word ran to and fro between Hannah and myself, it flickered like restless flame among my congregation . . .

His eyes flickered to and fro; his voice was very quiet, like a man unwillingly revealing secrets.

—We burned with vocation, the sun and the moon shone with His body of meaning, the people and the cities in the pictures on our walls seemed to burn in flames that did not consume them, the air itself with which I spoke was a flame that came leaping out of my mouth . . .

—Was this restlessness truly God?

—The space between ourselves and between all persons was threaded with swift messengers, and we knew this abundance was inexhaustible, it so overflowed that we had abundance to hand, to give to all the people we knew . . .

—Such proved not to be the case.

—It is changed. My parishioners (they know not what they do) divide me, eat me, drink me, and God replenishes me too slowly.

—You should retreat.

—I have taken a mistress!

—Is she a young woman?

—Yes. She is the young mother of the dead child.

—That will surely make matters worse. Is your wife ignorant of what you have done?

—She guesses, since God has come back to our lives.

—Is it the same God as before?

—This God . . . have you ever lit a match in thunder, in lightning?

From the Reflections of Mr Glass

White globe of rain, we are caught
In the drenching hair of the comet.

She mutters through the oak-crown, step by step,
Stair by green stair of fretted whispering leaves
Gathering her gowns about her, with their leaf-smell

She drags her wet white skirts across the lake
Into the green hills of oak trees, her wardrobes
Of many forms, many voices

She is never still, man cannot hold her

What if he could, glass-snake, waterfall
That has uttered the same sound since the mountain
Began, many mountains, many falls of water

Gynoecium of water, bursting rain-fruit
Packed with glass seeds, each whispering with its speed,
Harem, I walk to the river's source,
I looked up at the clouds

Mr Glass, what do you expect
When you plant the transparent apple-seed?

A glass apple-tree.
With crystal fruit.

Bite into it.

Glass juice runs
I am poisoned!
I am complete crystal!

The sun shines within you
Chains of yellow buds, briars;
Angry, you focus it along your arm in rays
That strike where you point, Fulminans!
In the dark you are a waiting seed,
However dark it is, there is enough light
To gather within your darkness like a seed of light

The man who arrests me becomes transparent!
The man who shoots me becomes transparent!
The woman who loves me becomes transparent!

Index of Titles and First Lines